THE ASSERTIVENESS WORKBOOK

How to Express Your Ideas
and Stand Up for Yourself
at Work and in Relationships

Randy J. Paterson, Ph.D.

New Harbinger Publications, Inc.

Publisher's Note

Copyright © 2000 by Randy Patterson
New Harbinger Publications, Inc.
5674 Shattuck Avenue
Oakland, CA 94609

Cover design by SHELBY DESIGNS AND ILLUSTRATES
Edited by Jueli Gastwirth
Text design by Tracy Marie Powell

Library of Congress Catalog Card Number: 00-134792
ISBN 1-57224-209-4 Paperback

New Harbinger Publications' Web site address: www.newharbinger.com

08   07   06

15   14   13   12   11   10

For Geoff

CONTENTS

ACKNOWLEDGMENTS

This workbook is based, in part, on a group assertiveness training program, entitled "Being There," that was developed for the Changeways Program at Vancouver Hospital and Health Sciences Centre in Vancouver, British Columbia. Many people were involved in the development of this program and deserve thanks. Rosanne Wozny participated in client recruitment and assessment and has assisted in the development of the program from its inception. Shelley van Etten, Martin Carroll, and Lindsey Jack all provided invaluable feedback on the program and helped structure some of the exercises that have found their way into this workbook. Elizabeth Eakin assisted on the clerical side with the preparation of materials—and by keeping us all organized.

Merv Gilbert at Vancouver Hospital has been extremely supportive of the Changeways program and of my work generally. To him, my thanks. I would also like to thank Bill Newby and Richard W. J. Neufeld for their strong, valued, and lasting impact on my career and my work. Jueli Gastwirth at New Harbinger Publications provided invaluable feedback in the preparation of this book, for which I am very grateful.

Finally, our clients at Changeways have assisted immeasurably through their participation in early versions of the program, tolerance for the challenges of program development, feedback about exercises and material that worked and did not work, support for the project, and inspiration and anecdotes. This manual could not have been written without their help.

INTRODUCTION

BEING THERE

Two kinds of people pick up books on assertiveness. Some want to polish their image. They have a face they present to the world, and sometimes it cracks. Sometimes the mask falls off. Sometimes people see through it. They want to learn how to hold the mask more firmly, how to present it more rigidly, how to prevent others from seeing them so easily. They have rejected themselves, and they have decided that they want to preserve the personality (or lack of it) that they display to the world. Often they want to learn how to control others more effectively. How to push others to agree with them, see their way of doing things, do it their way.

Some of the skills in this book may help these people in their quest. But the book isn't written for them. At least, it's not written to help them in the way they want to be helped.

Assertiveness isn't about building a good disguise. It's about developing the courage to take the disguise off. It's designed to help the other group of people. The ones who have already tried wearing a mask and have found they can't breathe very well with it on. They want to go out into the world naked-faced, as themselves, but not defenseless. They want to be themselves in a way that doesn't push others off-stage. In a way that invites the people they meet to be more fully themselves too.

Assertiveness, then, is about *being there*.

Many people in today's society fear conflict and criticism. They believe that in any conflict they would lose and that any criticism would crush them. They feel that they have no right to impose their views—or for that matter, themselves—on the world. They have been trained from childhood to believe that their role is to accept and live up to the standards that other people impose. Being visible, being flawed, holding opinions, or having wishes of their own all leave them open to attack.

Is this you?

The solution is to be invisible. To offer no opinion until others have done so, and then only to agree. To go along with any request. To impose no boundaries or barriers. To prevent yourself from ever saying "no." To give up on directing your own life. To pacify those who might disapprove of you. To hide your ideas, your dreams, your wishes, and your emotions. To dress, act, and live in order to blend into the background and disappear. To exist not so much as a person, but as a mirror for other people: reflecting back *their* ideas, *their* wishes, *their* expectations, *their* hopes, and *their* goals. To reflect and thereby vanish. Anything to keep yourself from really *being there*.

Unfortunately, this solution does not really work. Humans are not meant to be invisible, nor to live as reflections of the lives of others. Extinguishing the self is not an option. It leads to greater fear, more helplessness, sharper resentment, and deeper depression.

Other people see life as little more than a competition. If they are not to become invisible themselves, then others will have to be invisible. There is no choice. Their views must be accepted. Their wishes must be honored. Their way must be everyone's way. And should anyone not give in, the anger will flow. The issue will be forced, and the wishes, hopes, and desires of others will be ignored or trampled. To *be there*, other people (with their inconvenient attitudes and opinions) will have to be absent.

Is this you?

The competitive approach doesn't work either. The anger is never really satisfied. When others give in, it is never joyfully. And they begin drifting away to the exits, leaving the angry person alone to resent the desertion. The effort to control others makes life uncontrollable.

The real solution? To *be there*. Not to be perfect. To expose our flaws, our irrational emotions and opinions, our strange preferences, our incomprehensible dreams, our unaccountable tastes, and our all-too-human selves to others. To *be there*. Not so that others will bow down to us or hide themselves from us, but in a way that invites others to be there as well. A way that acknowledges the right of everyone to be every bit as irrational, flawed, and human as we are.

Assertiveness is all about *being there*.

In this workbook you will learn about many of the basic skills and ideas involved in being more fully present in your world and your life. Many of these skills you already know. Some may be new. Bringing them into your life will take practice and effort.

Ready?

Don't Read This Book

Perhaps you are wondering what good reading this book will do you. Let's end the suspense early. Not much. Perhaps you will learn more about assertiveness. You may recognize assertive strategies in others more readily. You may become more able to classify your own behavior as assertive or otherwise.

And neither your behavior nor your life will change.

Take a minute to think. What are you doing here? Why are you holding this book in your hand? If it is to *understand* more about assertiveness, then by all means read on. And just read. That'll be enough.

But perhaps you are dissatisfied with your way of dealing with people. Perhaps something holds you back from being yourself with others; from expressing your opinions, desires, or expectations; from setting boundaries that you can defend. Or perhaps it is hard for you to tolerate differences in others or to hold back from trying to control them. Maybe you find yourself overwhelmed by fear, anger, frustration, or despair when you have to deal with some of the most important people in your life.

If this sounds more like it, then *don't read this book*. Reading won't be enough. Throughout the book you will find a series of self-assessments, short writing exercises, and practice suggestions. Stop. Find a pen. Do the work. Carry out the practice exercises. Doing so will involve a greater investment on your part, but it will almost certainly generate a much greater return.

If being more assertive is important to you, it will have to be a high priority in your life. Is this the time for it? Are you able—and willing—to spend the time that it may take to change your style? If not, then maybe you should put this book on your "To Read" shelf and wait until you're really ready. You'll get to it. Sooner or later, your life will convince you that you need to be able to stand up for yourself, to *be* yourself, and to do so in a way that invites others to be themselves as well.

Does Anyone Else Want to Work with You?

You may be reading this book as part of an assertiveness training group. If not, don't worry. You will still be able to carry out most of the exercises and suggestions. You may wish, though, to see if anyone wants to work on this material with you. That way you can practice some of the techniques together. The feedback you give each other can be invaluable. It's always easier to learn these skills in practice sessions before you try them out in real life. Fake insults, for example, are a lot easier to handle than the real thing.

If you don't know anyone who wants to work on their own assertiveness, maybe you know someone who would still be willing to help you out with the exercises. Maybe asking them will be your first assignment for yourself. You may be surprised how agreeable they'd be. After all, you'll be practicing with them anyway—whether they know it or not.

Using Yourself as a Partner

One of the best sources of feedback you can have is yourself. Whether or not you are working with someone else, recruit *yourself* as a partner. Carry out some of the exercises in front of a mirror. Yes, that includes talking to yourself as though you were speaking to someone else. Although it's hard to be objective with ourselves, mirror practice can be a helpful way of evaluating how you come across. As you watch your performance, try to forget that you are looking at yourself. Imagine that it's someone else talking to you. How would you react?

Tape recorders and video cameras can also be immensely helpful. You can record your practice sessions and play them back. Then you can concentrate on evaluating your style. This is easier than trying to express yourself and evaluate your performance at the same time.

Assertiveness Scorecards

Luckily, you don't have to wait for the exercises in this workbook to practice assertiveness. Difficult interactions happen to most of us fairly often. You can take advantage of these situations by recording what happened and how you handled it and then working out a more assertive alternative. Coming up with what you would *like* to have done may take some time when you're getting started. But gradually you'll speed up. Eventually you will find that you come up with the assertive response right there, on the spot.

At the back of the workbook (see page 206), you will find a set of pages entitled "Assertiveness Scorecards." You have our permission to photocopy these pages for your own use. In fact, we recommend that you run off twenty or more copies for yourself. If anyone objects because they think you are violating our copyright, just show them this page—or come up with something suitably assertive of your own.

Then get to work. Use one form for each challenging interaction you have, *starting now*. Record your behavior in the situation and classify it as assertive, passive, aggressive, or passive-aggressive (using the definitions you will find in chapter 1). If it was other than assertive, come up with an alternative response that might have worked better.

Here's an example:

Date: *March 12*   Time: *3 pm*   Place: *My office*

Person/Situation: *Paul, my department head, asked me to hire his nephew for the summer replacement position, despite the fact that we need someone with experience.*

Your Response: *Couldn't think of what to say. Told him I'd think about it, then thanked him for the suggestion!*

Assertive, Passive, Aggressive, or P/A? *Passive.*

How did it turn out? *He expects me to hire the guy.*

Feelings Afterward: *Anger at myself. Anger at Paul for trying to manipulate me.*

Alternative Response: *Paul, we need someone in that position who knows the business. I've been planning to hire a student from the last year of the community college program. Your nephew is welcome to apply, but I'm not willing to put him at the head of the list unless he has the qualifications.*

As you use these forms you will find that you gradually become better and better at coming up with assertive responses. And as you read this workbook you will be able to apply the concepts discussed to your own life. Eventually the more effective responses will occur to you right in the situation, and you will be able to put them into practice.

Notice what you will have done. You will have made unwelcome situations welcome. They are no longer threats or disappointments. They are opportunities.

A Caution about Violent Relationships

Some people find themselves in violent relationships—sometimes with family members, sometimes with others. Many of these people believe that assertiveness training might help them to deal with the violence of others or reduce the temptation to engage in violence themselves. They may be right. But these problems deserve more specialized attention than a workbook such as this one can provide.

If violence plays a part in any of your relationships, you are urged not to regard this book as the solution. Instead, please address these issues with a counselor. If you are reading this manual as part of an assertiveness training group, please let your leader know that you have this additional concern.

One reason that *The Assertiveness Workbook* may be inappropriate for violent relationships is that you will be encouraged to deal with troublesome situations directly and assertively as you feel ready for them. Assertive strategies are designed to help you maintain control over your own life while letting go of attempting to control others. If someone close to you is violent, they may be threatened by your efforts to take back control over your life. Unless this is dealt with carefully, some violence on their part may follow.

If you have a history of violence yourself, then trying to practice being assertive with others may put you in "trigger situations" that cause you to escalate into violence without meaning to do so. Specialized help will be needed to reduce this risk. Please seek help to deal with this issue.

Organization of This Book

Which parts of this workbook should you use? Probably all of it. Most people will find that at least part of each chapter applies to their own situation. There may be certain areas, however, in which you have particular difficulty. You will want to pay special attention to the chapters on those topics.

Part One

Entitled "Understanding Assertiveness," Part One covers most of the concepts involved in being assertive. Chapter 1 defines the four primary communication styles: assertive, passive, aggressive, and passive-aggressive. Because these definitions form the keystone of everything that follows, you should be sure to read this chapter. It includes exercises designed to help you determine which of the styles you use the most and which situations you find most difficult. It also presents reasons why the assertive style usually works better than the alternatives.

If it's true that assertiveness leads to better outcomes in most situations, why isn't everyone assertive all the time? Unfortunately, it's not that easy. Being assertive requires 1) that you have some very specific skills and 2) that you use these skills when it is appropriate to do so. Even when you have the right skills, something may hold you back. Chapters 2 through 4 describe the barriers to assertive behavior.

Chapter 2 reviews the impact of stress on communication and how the stress response actually pulls us away from using the assertive style. Suggestions are provided on how to reduce stress in your life and overcome stress-related barriers to effective communication.

Chapter 3 discusses how the expectations of others can make it more difficult for us to be assertive. Over the years you may have unintentionally led others to expect nonassertive behavior from you, and they may react less favorably than you might think to the changes you want to make. Chapter 3 also considers the effect of your gender on others' expectations.

In chapter 4 you are invited to consider your own belief system and how it might impose barriers to assertiveness. Becoming aware of self-defeating beliefs is an essential step toward discarding them. You might never behave assertively until you have surmounted the belief barrier.

Chapter 5 suggests a series of positive, supportive beliefs for you to consider. These beliefs are associated with assertive action and can assist in guiding your decisions about the way that you communicate.

Once you have dealt with the barriers to assertive behavior, you are ready to begin practicing the skills involved. But first, chapter 6 provides a checklist of some last-minute concepts, tips, and guiding principles to take with you on the journey.

Part Two

Part Two is entitled "Becoming Assertive" and focuses on the actual skills used in assertive communication. Each chapter in this section includes one or more practical exercises designed to help you to master the skills. It will be important for you to make these exercises a priority if you really want to develop your ability to communicate in an assertive way.

Nonverbal communication tells others about our expectations, attitudes, and level of confidence. Even the best assertive communication can be undermined by a poor nonverbal style. Chapter 7 reviews the various elements of nonverbal behavior and compares the assertive, passive, and aggressive styles (the passive-aggressive style typically mimics passive nonverbal behavior). A series of exercises provides strategies for honing an assertive nonverbal style.

Are you able to express your opinion effectively while leaving room for others to think differently? This essential relationship skill lies at the heart of the concept of being present with others and is discussed in chapter 8.

Chapters 9 through 12 consider the issues of providing and receiving feedback in relationships. Chapter 9 opens the topic by considering a skill that seems simple but is a surprisingly frequent source of difficulty: receiving compliments. Some of the most common traps are covered, along with the distorted thinking underlying them.

Next, we consider the giving of positive feedback. Most people are stingier with positive feedback than they need to be, and this reluctance is motivated by a variety of fears. Chapter 10 challenges these ideas and provides specific recommendations for giving positive feedback that is useful to the person receiving it.

In chapter 11 the value of negative feedback is discussed, along with the difficulty of gleaning useful information from the criticism we receive. Suggestions are made for defusing the anger that frequently accompanies negative feedback, as well as for narrowing criticism to the real issue at hand.

Chapter 12 covers behavior that many people avoid and that most others cannot perform effectively: giving negative (or constructive) feedback. Strategies are given for providing such feedback in a way that is useful and not hurtful. The accompanying practice exercises are designed to increase your comfort with these situations.

Who's in charge of your life? Chapter 13 argues that if you aren't able to say "no" then it certainly isn't you. The ability to refuse unreasonable requests is an essential skill of self-determination. This chapter considers the fears that hold people back and provides a set of skills involved in setting and maintaining personal boundaries.

Chapter 14 puts the shoe on the other foot by discussing strategies for making requests of others. Some people avoid making requests altogether, while others make demands rather than requests. A structured four-step strategy for phrasing requests is presented, plus a set of exercises designed to increase your confidence and comfort in translating your plans into action.

All of the skills in the book come into play when you find yourself in difficult conflict-laden situations. The final two chapters deal with confrontation. Chapter 15 argues that confrontation is an essential though sometimes painful aspect of almost any close relationship and that adequate preparation on your part can make confrontations go much more smoothly. It provides a ten-step preparation strategy that considers issues such as defining the real problem, envisioning your goal, assessing your own responsibilities, and choosing your time and setting. Chapter 16 deals with the confrontation itself and presents fifteen strategies for keeping the discussion on topic and moving toward a solution.

Throughout, remember that this is a workbook. You will find self-assessments, exercises, practice session advice, and so on. These are essential elements in learning to be more assertive. So let's get started. Based on the description of the book given above, which chapters do you think will be the most critical for you to work on?

List the chapters here:

_____

_____

_____

Don't use this as a cue to ignore the remaining chapters, however. Each chapter builds on the one before it, so you will probably want to read them all. Take special care with the chapters you have identified. Reread them as necessary and ensure that you carry out the associated practice exercises.

Throughout your reading of the book, continue to fill out Assertiveness Scorecards for the difficult exchanges you experience. As time passes, you may begin to find that these situations become easier and easier to handle.

PART ONE

UNDERSTANDING ASSERTIVENESS

CHAPTER 1

WHAT IS ASSERTIVENESS?

Human beings are social animals. We constantly communicate with each other. Sometimes to ask directions to the nearest grocery store; sometimes to ask for a date; sometimes to communicate displeasure; sometimes to offer a compliment; sometimes to resolve disputes; sometimes to turn down requests; sometimes to accept.

Assertiveness is a style of communication that can be used in all of these situations. But it is only one of four such styles. The other three are the *passive* style, the *aggressive* style, and the *passive-aggressive* style.

Each of these styles is used for a variety of reasons. In most situations, the assertive style is the most effective of the four. Unfortunately, most people do not use the assertive style as often as they could. As a result, their interactions with other people are frustrating and unsatisfying.

Let's take a look at each of the styles in turn. As you read them over, you may find yourself trying to see which description fits you the best. This can be useful. Most people use one of the styles more than the others. But remember that the styles are types of *communication*, not types of *people*. All of us use each of the four styles at least some of the time. Try to think of the times that you have used each one.

The Passive Style

Nadia looked exhausted. She had been referred to a psychologist for symptoms of anxiety and depression. Both were clearly visible on her face. Distressed people sometimes have a convincing mask of confidence that they can present to the world, hiding what they are experiencing. If Nadia had ever had such a mask, it was cracking badly.

She described her life. She held a full-time job as a clerk in a small accounting firm and lived in a suburb with her husband and son. Her mother, who lived across town, was healthy, but she depended on Nadia for everything: drives to appointments, decisions about purchases, what to wear, yard work, chores about the house, everything. Nadia's sisters helped very little and indeed were cut off from her. They criticized her for helping their mother so much and openly accused her of angling for a larger inheritance.

Nadia's home was no retreat from the stress of the world. Her husband's only contribution was to pick up the newspaper—so that he could read it. She described her eleven-year-old son as the joy of her life but lamented the fact that her other duties meant she could not care for him as well as he seemed to need. There was his laundry to do, his bed to make, his room to tidy, his favorite meals to cook, and when she failed to do things exactly right, he pouted and became disappointed with her. She could see why. After all, wasn't it a mother's duty to take proper care of her son?

Work was stressful. She was the only clerical assistant in the firm and could barely keep ahead of the tide of work and tasks constantly coming her way. She harbored a fearful knowledge of her own incompetence. She was thankful that her employers hadn't yet caught on to the fact that she was struggling. Each time she completed a job they would give her two more. She knew that someday soon she would simply be incapable of getting it all done and they would be shocked to find the imposter in their midst. On top of everything, they never seemed to think to give her a raise. She guessed that she didn't deserve one.

At one point, Nadia began to weep with anxiety and frustration, saying that she felt her life was unmanageable. She wanted to be convinced otherwise, but she was right: things really were as bad as she described. It was no wonder she felt anxious and depressed. She had become a servant to the world. She did nothing that was just for her and had stopped living her own life so long ago that she no longer knew what she might want to do even if she could find the time to do it. Although she accomplished prodigious amounts of work and had developed innumerable skills in the process, she could take pride in none of it, because she secretly felt herself to be a failure and an imposter.

Nadia is an excellent example of someone who overuses the passive style. Many of her problems were situational: a stressful life at work, demanding relations, an unsatisfying marriage, a difficult child. Her reaction to these stressors, however, was to deny her frustration, take personal responsibility for all of the problems, and hope that things would get better. Instead, her behavior appeared to be making things worse.

The passive style is designed to avoid conflict at all costs. We do this by:

- Giving in to unreasonable demands from others.

"The overnight shift? The day after my wedding? Um, well, sure, OK. No, no trouble at all."

- Going along with the crowd.

"Bob's Ptomaine Shack for dinner? Oh, uh, yeah, that sounds like a great place!"

- Not offering your opinion until others have offered theirs.

"My opinion on capital punishment . . . well, what do you think? For jaywalkers? Oh, well, yes, I'd go along with that."

- Never criticizing or giving negative feedback.

"I got your (two-sentence) budget report yesterday. No, the crayon was just fine. No problem at all."

- Never doing or saying anything that might attract comment or disapproval.

"No one will notice me if I wear these pants. Perfect. I'll buy them."

The result of the passive style: We give control over our lives to other people—even when we don't want to do so.

In wolf packs there is an established order of dominance between the animals. When two wolves meet, the less dominant one will behave as though to say, *"Yes, you are more important than I am. I submit to you. Don't attack me."* When we use the passive style we behave in much the same way. Like submissive wolves, we may avoid eye contact, appear nervous, look downward, and make ourselves small. We can think of the passive style as a posture of submission to others.

Calling this style "passive" can be misleading. It suggests that the person just sits around saying nothing. Sometimes this is exactly what happens. But, like Nadia, a person using a passive style is often *more* active than anyone else: scurrying around, working twice as hard as others, explaining his or her actions, trying desperately to gain approval, and striving to solve everyone else's problems.

All of us can think of certain situations in which we would willingly hand the lead over to others. The first time we go mountain climbing we might be quite happy to have an expert give us orders. In fact, it would be alarming to have the climbing instructor ask *us* what to do. In some circumstances, it is just fine to take a secondary or submissive position. We can *choose* to use a less assertive style.

Beliefs That Hold You Back

We always have the choice of whether or not to be passive. But often we are not aware of making the choice. Instead, when we behave passively, we often feel helpless, as though we are not in charge of our own lives. This is because passive behavior often results from a belief that we are not *allowed* to behave any other way. Here are some examples of beliefs that may hold you back:

- "Other people are more important than I am."

- "Other people are entitled to have control over their lives. I'm not."

- "They can do things effectively. I can't."

- "My role in life is to be the servant."

Passive Emotions

There are a lot of emotions that support the passive style. For example:

- A profound fear of being rejected. If you don't do everything others want, will they still like you?

- Helplessness and frustration at the lack of control over your life. Psychologist Martin Seligman (1991) argues that a sense of helplessness is a primary risk factor for the development of depression. People who rely exclusively on the passive style really *are* helpless, because they cannot override the demands of others. As a result, the helplessness may escalate into discouragement, a sense of futility, or even all-out depression.

- Resentment at all of the demands being made on you. If you find yourself thinking that many of your friends are manipulative "users," perhaps it is really you who created the situation by adopting a passive style that actually *encourages* others to use you.

How Does the Passive Style Develop?

There are a lot of reasons why people adopt a mainly passive style.

- Some people grow up in extremely considerate families. *"Oh, don't ask Jane to do that; she's busy enough already."* As a result, they never get any practice saying *"no."*

- Some children are taught to be perfectly obedient. Although obedience to others may be useful during childhood, we all need to rethink this style when we become adults.

- In some families, children's requests, needs, or boundaries are never respected. Why would you ever become assertive if it never works?

- In some families, assertiveness unfortunately leads to violence. *"How dare you say 'no' to me! I'll show you!"*

- Some people just never see assertiveness in action. All they see as they grow up is aggression or passivity. And if you've never seen it, it's hard to imagine what assertiveness would be like.

Nadia, it turned out, had a number of these influences. She grew up in a family with a tyrannical father and a passive mother. Her father demanded absolute obedience and her mother modeled it. She rarely saw assertiveness in action. As a child, whenever Nadia had tried to assert her independence, she had been punished for it. As the eldest daughter, she was expected to care for her younger sisters.

The passive style can be useful at times. As the only option, however, it generally leads to misery.

The Aggressive Style

"No offense, but you just don't understand business," Mike said.

Mike was taking exception to the suggestion that his aggressiveness was doing more harm than good in his life. Mike ran a car dealership and had about thirty employees. He dressed well and had a look of confident success about him. What he couldn't disguise was the fact that he was in a psychologist's office, sent there by an ultimatum from his wife. She was threatening to leave him.

Mike was dissatisfied with his life but felt that his problems were due to circumstance. Business was tight, suppliers were pushy and incompetent, and it was impossible to find employees who didn't need a fire lit under them now and then. As a result, Mike frequently found himself losing his temper at work. He would order his employees around, telling them that they didn't know their jobs. He would shout himself hoarse at least twice a day dealing with suppliers over the phone. And twice recently, he'd angrily ordered important customers out of his office. His staff seemed secretive, turnover was high, and he was beginning to feel the business slipping away from him.

As Mike put it, he had a hard time leaving work at work. At home he behaved in the same angry, demanding manner with his wife and children. Although never physically abusive, he had come perilously close on several occasions. When he wasn't yelling, his anger came out in other ways. He'd impose a "communication embargo" on one or another family member, flatly refusing to speak to them for days on end. He was rigid and authoritarian on disciplinary matters with the children. He was insulting and definitive whenever he expressed his own views, and his wife stated that he was sarcastic and dismissive of her opinions.

As he spoke about his life, Mike began to reveal his fears. He knew that his family was beginning to work around him, communicating behind his back as a way of avoiding his anger. He clearly loved his wife and children but was acutely aware of the dangers of the world. If he didn't protect them, who would? He felt deep discomfort when he saw any member of the family doing, saying, or even thinking anything that he did not agree with. It felt like a loss of control. And if he didn't have control, what might happen?

The situation seemed unlikely to continue, however. If business didn't start going better, the company would go under. If he didn't change his style, he was going to lose his family, too.

Mike overused the aggressive style. Similar to most people with this manner, he saw his behavior as the product of his situation—an *effect*. He was less aware that his behavior was also a cause; specifically, the cause of many of his problems. Although his style made him look frightening and powerful, it originated, as aggression almost always does, in fear. Mike had a profound fear of what would happen if he was not in control of everyone around him. The aggression was designed to assert control. But as often happens, it was having the effect of causing control to slip away from him.

The aggressive style is the flip side of the passive style. Instead of submitting to others, we try to get others to submit to us. It is important for us to win, regardless of the cost to other people. Our aim is to control the behavior of others through intimidation. Their opinions, boundaries, goals, and requests are stupid or meaningless—barriers to be overcome. We are dominant wolves, bending others to our will.

The funny thing is that aggressive people usually don't feel all that dominant. Instead, they often feel helpless, abused, and the subject of unreasonable and excessive demands. Aggression is almost always the result of feeling threatened. Responding with anger seems perfectly justified.

The Advantages of Aggression

Aggressive behavior is usually ineffective for achieving one's goals in the long run. But in the short term, there are some advantages to the aggressive style:

- Intimidating others into doing what you want *may* get things done for a while (though eventually people will resent you, have little incentive to do things well, and feel little affection or loyalty toward you).

- If others fear you, they may make fewer demands (though they will also make fewer pleasant invitations—and if you were more assertive, you could deal with their unpleasant demands confidently).

- Being aggressive can make you feel powerful (though it makes others feel *worse* and the feeling of power lasts only for a short time, usually followed by more frustration and helplessness).

- Aggression can seem like a good way of getting even for past wrongs done to you (though it usually starts an unpleasant exchange that leaves neither person feeling "even"; and, chances are, you will wind up worse off than you were before).

- Sometimes it feels like you need to blow off steam (though the research suggests that "blowing off steam" makes you *more* angry—not less—in the long run).

After behaving aggressively, the feeling of power and justification usually fades quickly. In its place come guilt for hurting the feelings of others, shame at not being able to deal with situations and people more rationally, and reduced self-esteem. Sometimes these consequences are covered over by long and angry self-justifications for the behavior (*"they really deserved it, because . . ."*). But the situation has usually been made worse, not better. The disagreement between you and the other person is still there, and now they resent you for behaving badly toward them.

Why Do People Act Aggressively?

How does the aggressive style develop? Here are just a few possibilities:

- Having an aggressive parent who serves as a model for you.

"I guess that's the way to act if you want something."

- Low self-esteem that causes you to feel threatened by minor difficulties.

"I can't handle this situation unless I intimidate the other person into silence."

- Initial experiences of obtaining what you want through aggression.

"Hey, it worked with Mom—I've gotta try this more often!"

- Failing to see the negative consequences of aggression.

"I wonder why she's been so emotionally distant ever since I convinced her to see my way? Maybe it's time I got angry with her again."

Mike had grown up in a family somewhat like Nadia's: with an aggressive father and a passive mother. He had borne the brunt of his father's anger and had responded by behaving in much the same way with others. Around his father he felt small and powerless. He was determined to avoid feeling that way with anyone else. He would feel anxious whenever anyone had any kind of power over him, and he would defend himself with rage. Suppliers, employees, and family members all had the potential to affect him, and so they each were potential targets for his aggression.

The Passive-Aggressive Style

"Damn, I forgot them again," said Alan.

Like the week before, Alan had forgotten to bring in the questionnaires he'd been given two weeks previously and that he'd said he had filled out. No matter. The questionnaires weren't essential, and a picture was beginning to emerge without them.

It was clear that Alan was depressed. What was also clear was that Alan experienced a profound fear of others, which he could acknowledge—and considerable anger, which he couldn't.

An unassuming man in his late forties, Alan worked in the public sector as a civil servant. He hated working for the government and dwelt on the office politics that swept through his department on every issue from promotions and important policy matters to who got the corner cubicles near the windows. As he discussed the office atmosphere with his psychotherapist, it became clear that he was intensely caught up in the politics himself. At times he would smile as he reported some background maneuvering he had done that had been successful.

Alan was intensely sarcastic about the managers of the department. When asked whether he had ever raised any of his issues with them, he said that he hadn't. It was no use, for one thing, and he became tongue-tied and incoherent, for another. It was better, he said, to work "behind the scenes." Some tasks could safely be ignored. Others could be done in such a way that you wouldn't be asked to do them again. And you could always relieve your frustration by talking with your coworkers about the person giving you grief.

His strategizing had not seemed to work as well as he'd wished, however. Alan had repeatedly been passed over for promotion, despite knowing more about the organization than anyone else. Though he was prized for his inside knowledge by some of his coworkers, he was emotionally close to none of them and held a lingering resentment toward those who slighted him.

His private life was also unsatisfactory. He'd remained single since getting a divorce in his late twenties. He was profoundly lonely but feared rejection. He knew one of his best traits was his wickedly funny sense of humor, but he also knew that he sometimes used it to keep people at arm's length. His friendships didn't seem to last.

Although he denied being a particularly angry person, Alan did admit to being disappointed by others and to feeling resentful about some of the things that had happened to him. He could never bring himself to express his views honestly to the people involved, however. What if they got angry? What if they retaliated? No, it was better to keep a lid on his frustrations.

Alan was a master of the passive-aggressive style. He experienced intense anger but had difficulty acknowledging it even to himself. Instead, anger became "disappointment" or "frustration." He was intensely fearful of the consequences of stating his point of view directly. As a result, he seldom declined unwelcome projects or spoke openly about his workload. Instead, he would adopt an indirect strategy that would get him his way without necessitating an open and candid discussion. This strategy enabled him to attack others without ever having to take responsibility for his behavior.

As the name suggests, the passive-aggressive style combines elements of both the passive and the aggressive styles. The anger of the aggressive style and the fear of the passive style both have an influence. The anger makes you want to "get" the other person, but the fear holds you back from doing it directly. When we are passive-aggressive we disguise our aggression so that we can avoid taking responsibility for it.

Consider an example. Your employer has asked for a report by noon Friday, despite the fact that you are already overloaded with work. Rather than yelling at her (aggressive), staying all night to finish it (passive), or explaining the situation (assertive), you simply "forget" to do the report. You get your way, frustrate the boss, and remain able to deny responsibility for your actions (after all, *anyone* can forget things now and then).

Here are some more examples of passive-aggressive behavior:

- Undermining coworkers by bad-mouthing them to the boss.

- "Accidentally" dropping a can of paint all over the basement floor.

- Not being able to find time to do the favor you promised.

- Routinely showing up late for appointments, always with an excuse in hand.

- Developing a "headache" just when you were supposed to go to your spouse's office party.

- Doing a household chore badly enough that someone else takes over.

In all cases you get your own way, but you have a plausible excuse that allows you to escape taking responsibility for your actions. You manage to avoid being confronted by others who are affected. If they try to confront you, you can always deny any intent (*"No, I really* wanted *to be on time, but the bus was late"*).

Not every mistake, missed appointment, or late arrival is passive-aggressive. Some people really are busy, sometimes we really do forget, and some jobs really are unexpectedly difficult. The question is whether at some level we *intended* the bad outcome to happen.

This can be hard to figure out. We may think our intentions were honorable. But was there a hint of satisfaction when things went wrong? Do we *routinely* do the same things, even though they always turn out awkwardly for someone else? Are we almost *always* late? Do we *repeatedly* take on projects that we should know we will never complete? If so, we may be using a passive-aggressive style without knowing it.

The passive-aggressive style is based on a misperception: the idea that there are no consequences of deniable aggression. But there are. Eventually others begin to see us as unreliable, irresponsible, disorganized, or inconsiderate. Although they may never be able to point to specific examples, their general opinion of us will decline. In Alan's case, he began to get passed over for promotion.

The emotional consequences combine the worst of both the passive and aggressive styles. Self-esteem drops. Anxiety builds because we never know when someone will see through our passivity and confront us. We feel that we are not in control of our own lives. And shame and guilt can build up from constantly letting others down.

The Origin of the Passive-Aggressive Style

Where does the passive-aggressive style come from? Usually the person who overuses this style has a history that includes elements of both the passive and the aggressive styles. They experience significant anger and a desire for control, but they fear the consequences of expressing themselves directly. Openly assertive or aggressive behavior may have been punished in the past. There may also be a desire for rescue. *"If I behave helplessly enough, surely someone will come and help me."*

Alan was the youngest in a large family. He got the attention of his parents and his older siblings, some of whom faintly resented his status as the baby and, therefore, star of the family show. He learned early that if he ever got into trouble someone would help him out or take over. This encouraged him to look more helpless than he really was. If others annoyed him, he would go behind their backs to get them into trouble or get his own way. His style served him well as a child. When he reached adulthood, however, this style turned out to be less effective.

The Assertive Style

None of the styles above is very satisfying. All have negative effects on our relationships. None involve an open and honest exchange in which everyone's wishes and desires are respected. Surely there is some way for us to be in a relationship without denying either others or ourselves. This is the goal of the assertive style.

Assertiveness is not a strategy for getting your own way. Instead, it recognizes that you are in charge of your own behavior and that *you* decide what you will and will not do. Similarly, the assertive style involves recognizing that other people are in charge of *their* own behavior and does not attempt to take that control from them. When we behave assertively, we are able to acknowledge our own thoughts and wishes honestly, without the expectation that others will automatically give in to us. We express respect for the feelings and opinions of others without necessarily adopting their opinions or doing what they expect or demand.

This does not mean that we become inconsiderate of the wishes of others. We listen to their wishes and expectations, then we decide whether or not to go along with them. We might choose to do so even if we would prefer to do something else. But it is *our* choice. Whenever we go along with others it is our decision to do so anyway. But we can often feel helpless because we forget that we are under our own control.

If we are being assertive we may also express our preferences for the behavior of others. We might assertively request that someone speak to us in a kinder way, or do a favor for us, or complete a task that they have undertaken. But we will acknowledge that whether they do any of these things is up to them—as indeed it is.

Assertiveness skills can be difficult to learn. Many of us grow up without learning to use them effectively. As well, assertiveness sometimes goes against our temptations. Sometimes we want to push other people to do our bidding. Sometimes we are desperately afraid of conflict. Assertiveness may mean holding ourselves back from our automatic ways of doing things. It doesn't come easily.

And yet assertiveness offers many benefits:

- It allows us to relate to others with less conflict, anxiety, and resentment.

- It allows us to be relaxed around others, because we know that we will be able to handle most situations reasonably well.

- It helps us to focus on the present situation, rather than allowing our communication to be contaminated by old resentments from the past (*"This is just like the time you . . ."*) or unrealistic fears about the future (*"I can't set a precedent by giving in . . ." "What if she takes this to mean . . ."*).

- It allows us to retain our self-respect without trampling that of others. Although it allows others to think whatever they want to think about us, it tends to build their respect for us as well.

- It increases self-confidence by reducing our attempts to live up to the standards of others and by reducing the need for approval.

- It acknowledges the right of other people to live their lives, with the result that they feel less resentment toward us for trying to control them.

- It gives us control over our own lives and, by reducing helplessness, assertiveness may reduce depression.

- It is the only strategy that really allows us and others to fully *be* in the relationship.

That's a fairly brief description of the assertive style, isn't it? Shouldn't it be spelled out a little more clearly? Well, yes. That's the topic of the rest of the book.

How Do the Styles Connect?

Some people think of assertiveness as a middle ground between passivity and aggressiveness. That is, some believe that assertiveness is more aggressive than the passive style but more passive than the aggressive style.

This leads some people to worry that they will "overshoot" when they try to become more assertive. Maybe they will become too aggressive (if they used to be too passive) or too passive (if they used to be aggressive). It also leaves us wondering where the passive-aggressive style fits in. Here's a better way of looking at it:

In this diagram the passive-aggressive style is shown as a combination of the passive style and the aggressive style. The assertive style is elevated above all

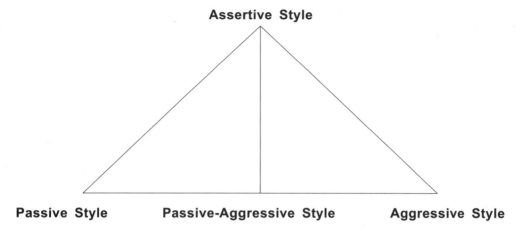

Assertive Style

Passive Style   **Passive-Aggressive Style**   **Aggressive Style**

of the rest to reflect the fact that it usually is the most effective. The lines show that the assertive style is distinct but related to all the others.

One More Style: The Alternator

"Sometimes I'm passive. Sometimes I'm aggressive. Does that make me passive-aggressive?"

Some people notice that they alternate between the passive and aggressive styles. Most of the time, they keep their opinions to themselves and behave passively. Then, every so often they explode with aggression. This is normal to an extent. Most of us use all of the styles at least some of the time. But some people find that they swing from passive to aggressive with some regularity. What's the problem here?

People who behave in this alternating style are *not* being passive-aggressive. The passive-aggressive style involves being both passive and aggressive *at the same time*. For example, being late means that you simultaneously inconvenience the other person (aggressive) while avoiding responsibility for your actions (passive).

The main problem for people who swing from the passive to the aggressive style is usually that they are too passive. They behave passively and they get frustrated. This is the normal result of being too passive. Eventually the frustration builds up until they cannot stand it anymore. The straw breaks the camel's back, so to speak, and then they explode. They have a huge aggressive outburst that looks like a temper tantrum. Then they go back to being passive—until the next time. People start to view those who act in this manner as ticking time bombs.

The solution for people who alternate is the same as for those who overuse each of the other styles: learn better assertiveness skills. If these individuals became more assertive, they would feel less frustration and helplessness. The pressure would not build up in the same way and they would not reach the point of exploding. Of course, a little stress management and anger control training wouldn't hurt either.

Checkpoint: Where Are You?

Again, most people use all of the styles. You are *already* assertive. And aggressive. And passive. And passive-aggressive. But you may be using one of the styles much more than the others. Which one?

To give you an idea, consult the table on the next page. There are four columns: one for each of the styles. There are five rows. These represent the behavior, nonverbal style, beliefs, emotions, and goals associated with each style.

In each row place a checkmark in the column that describes your usual style the best. When you are done, look to see which column has the most checkmarks. Although this is not a formal psychological assessment, there is a good chance that the style with the most checkmarks is the one you use most often.

Which Category Received the Most Checkmarks?

☐ **Passive.** Better assertiveness skills may be exactly what you need. It will be a good idea for you to pay special attention to chapters 2 through 5, which explore some of the barriers to assertive behavior. You probably have some negative beliefs about assertiveness that may be holding you back.

☐ **Aggressive.** This workbook may be very helpful for you. The material on tolerating differences and allowing others to control their own behavior (chapters 4, 5, and 14) may be particularly important. Pay special attention to the material on anger (particularly chapter 2).

☐ **Passive-Aggressive.** You may be able to pursue your needs and interests, but you have some difficulty being open about it. This difficulty may stem from a fear of conflict. The material on giving your opinion openly (chapter 8), saying "no" (chapter 13), and handling confrontations (chapters 15 and 16) may be particularly valuable for you.

☐ **Assertive.** Excellent. If the exercise is accurate, you may already be using your assertiveness skills much of the time. We can all learn more, however. As you go through the workbook, try to identify the skills that still give you trouble. Focus your efforts on these areas.

Three Journeys toward Assertiveness

Let's take a look back at the three case histories that began the sections on the passive, aggressive, and passive-aggressive styles. Each of these people made a personal commitment to learn better assertiveness skills. None found the task easy. Each found it valuable. If you saw parts of yourself in their histories, perhaps you will see parts of your future in their journeys.

	Passive	Aggressive	Passive-Aggressive	Assertive
Behavior	☐ Keep quiet. Don't say what you feel, need, or want. Put yourself down frequently. Apologize when you express yourself. Deny that you disagree with others or feel differently.	☐ Express your feelings and wants as though any other view is unreasonable or stupid. Dismiss, ignore, or insult the needs, wants, and opinions of others.	☐ Failure to meet the expectations of others through "deniable" means: forgetting, being delayed, and so on. Deny personal responsibility for your actions.	☐ Express your needs, wants, and feelings directly and honestly. Don't assume you are correct or that everyone will feel the same way. Allow others to hold other views without dismissing or insulting them.
Nonverbal	☐ Make yourself small. Look down, hunch your shoulders, avoid eye contact. Speak softly.	☐ Make yourself large and threatening. Eye contact is fixed and penetrating. Voice is loud, perhaps shouting.	☐ Usually mimics the passive style.	☐ Body is relaxed, movements are casual. Eye contact is frequent, but not glaring.
Beliefs	☐ Others' needs are more important than yours. They have rights; you don't. Their contributions are valuable. Yours are worthless.	☐ Your needs are more important and more justified than theirs. You have rights, they don't. Your contributions are valuable. Theirs are silly, wrong, or worthless.	☐ You are entitled to get your own way, even after making commitments to others. You are not responsible for your actions.	☐ Your needs and those of others are equally important. You have equal rights to express yourselves. You both have something valuable to contribute. You are responsible for your behavior.
Emotions	☐ Fear of rejection. Helplessness, frustration, and anger. Resentment toward others who "use" you. Reduced self-respect.	☐ Angry or powerful at the time, and victorious when you win. Afterward: remorse, guilt, or self-hatred for hurting others.	☐ Fear that you would be rejected if you were more assertive. Resentment at the demands of others. Fear of being confronted.	☐ You feel positive about yourself and the way you treat others. Self-esteem rises.
Goals	☐ Avoid conflict. Pleas others at any expense to yourself. Give others control over you.	☐ Win at any expense to others. Gain control over them.	☐ Get your own way without having to take responsibility.	☐ Both you and others keep your self-respect. Express yourself without having to win all the time. No one controls anyone else.

Nadia's Story—From Passive to Assertive

Nadia believed that the problems she faced were in the world around her. Her family and work were simply too demanding. To the extent that she saw herself as the problem, it was only that she was inadequate. She felt she always had been.

The idea that her communication style might be the cause of some of her life's distressing situations was a new one. And yet, when she reviewed each of the communication styles, she had little trouble identifying the one she used the most: the passive style. For a time, Nadia teetered on the edge of using this revelation as yet another way to undermine her own self-esteem. "Not only do I have all these problems, but I'm at fault for creating them!"

Then Nadia began to recognize where the style had come from. As the eldest daughter in a large family, responsibility for her sisters had fallen to her when her father became seriously ill and her mother had had to care for him. Nadia had seen it as her job to keep things together. She remembered once telling her mother that she wanted to go out with a boyfriend. Her exhausted mother had snapped that Nadia didn't care whether her father lived or died. Doing things for herself had seemed unforgivable after that. Life improved when she got married, but gradually she fell into her old style, taking on more and more responsibility and expressing herself less and less.

Nadia began by working on her relationship with her mother. By monitoring their discussions, Nadia realized, with shock, that her mother seldom asked her to do anything. She would talk about something that needed to be done, and Nadia would volunteer to do it. She never waited to be asked. She decided that her first change would be to stop volunteering. She would wait to be asked. At first, her mother's hints became more and more obvious, and, sure enough, she made a number of requests—but fewer than Nadia had expected. Her mother began doing some things for herself and reported seeing other people more often. Nadia began to wonder whether some of her "help" had actually undermined her mother's confidence and ability to do things for herself. She resolved to continue caring for her mother, but at the level that her mother actually needed.

At work, Nadia kept a record of her activities and was surprised to see how much she was really doing. She realized that no matter how efficient she became she would never be able to complete everything. She started the process of change by asking those who gave her work to prioritize the tasks. It didn't work. Everything was given top priority. As a result, she began giving estimates of when she could complete each task. If there were objections, she would offer to move a task up the priority list, ahead of other tasks from that same person. Her employers began to see that she was swamped with work. Eventually she asked for a meeting to review her job, and she presented her concerns. She expected to be fired at once. She wasn't. With better communication and clear feedback from her, things began to improve.

With her son, Nadia came to realize that her task as a mother was not only to provide support, but also to prepare him for independent life as an adult. Catering to him, requiring nothing, and accepting all of his demands and criticism were not helping. She stopped making his bed. She struggled to keep from giving in or justifying herself when he was critical. She placed a box in the basement and announced that she would put anything found on the floor or otherwise out of place in the box. At first her son was enraged and became even messier. Gradually he began to remember to pick up his things, however, and Nadia responded by easing up on the speed with which his possessions vanished into the basement.

She drew up a list of all of the chores that needed doing on a regular basis and convened a family meeting to ask for input on a reasonable division of responsibilities. Her son suggested that he be responsible for making his own bed (which in itself was a surprise) but that she should do almost everything else. She was able to state that this didn't seem fair to her. He reluctantly agreed to take on a few more tasks, which he promptly forgot to do. Nadia was able to keep herself from doing them instead and, as agreed, stopped making desserts and buying snack food. Slowly, shakily, things began to get back on track.

Her husband responded the same way, reluctantly agreeing to do more around the house, forgetting, and then gradually beginning to do some of them. It wasn't perfect, and the family went through a period of tension. It was a surprise to Nadia when the tension began to decline and the family began to get along better than they had before. She identified a few personal interests that she had not had the energy to pursue and began indulging them. She felt that she was getting her own life back after a long time.

By the end of therapy, Nadia did not have perfect assertiveness skills. But she didn't need them to be perfect. They were working reasonably well. As she continued to practice, she continued to improve.

Mike's Story—From Aggressive to Assertive

As long as Mike focussed on his anger and frustration with his work and family, he couldn't address the real problem. Once he began to see the fear that lay behind the anger (fear of losing his family and his business, fear of being left alone), he could see more clearly what needed to be done. He started out by keeping Assertiveness Scorecards (see the Introduction for more information) for every aggressive exchange, including the immediate and longer-term effects. He realized that he was right: his aggressive manner was effective. It got things done in the short-term. But when he looked at the impact on his emotions, the emotions of other people, and the longer-term outcomes, he realized that his style was failing badly.

Mike couldn't change his style overnight. He began by cutting down on his coffee and doing regular relaxation exercises. Then he identified a few specific suppliers to try out a new style on. At first, he communicated with them mainly by letter and email, which enabled him to think about what he was saying before delivering the message. He felt as though he was just suppressing his anger and play-acting being "nice." But he noticed that the new style was just as effective as his rants, and he didn't feel as embarrassed or guilty afterward. Next, he focused on changing his communication style with a few employees and experienced positive results. As the weeks passed, Mike began to notice that those suppliers and those employees were actually performing better than they had before. The atmosphere of tension around the car dealership began to subside ever so slightly. He had moments when he was actually having fun at work.

When he drove home, Mike would sit in his car in the garage and do a relaxation exercise before going into the house. It felt like a punctuation mark between his work and his home life, and he felt more able to distinguish between the two. He asked the family not to give him any issues to deal with for at least fifteen minutes after arriving home, and he was able to admit to them that it was because he was often tense. His Assertiveness Scorecards revealed the issues that tended to trigger his anger with his wife and children. When these issues came up he inserted a break before responding. His family teased him for taking so many walks around the block.

Things didn't change overnight. Mike and his wife attended several joint therapy sessions during which they would practice specific communication skills. In one of the exercises his wife would express an opinion that she knew he did not share, and he would slowly and painfully frame his response (including reflective listening and non-aggressively stating his own view) line-by-line, with many missteps along the way. His wife was installed temporarily as the sole disciplinarian in the house while he practiced his new skills. He worked at clarifying his own standards for his children's behavior. The family met to discuss the standards they agreed on and came up with specific consequences (none involving yelling) that would come into play if the rules were broken. Gradually, Mike was brought back into the process on an equal footing with his wife.

Mike had been so aggressive for so long that he feared he could never change. What he hadn't counted on was that the new style would have rewards that would help him keep going. The family home became a place that he enjoyed. Work improved. The feeling that everything was slipping away began to subside.

Alan's Story—From Passive-Aggressive to Assertive

Alan's predominantly passive-aggressive style had become so automatic that most of the time he didn't realize what he was doing. The style is intended to hide aggression from others, but it can also hide it from oneself. By reading about the passive-aggressive style and keeping Assertiveness Scorecards, Alan realized he was trying to attack others without being caught. He found this realization unflattering.

Like Nadia, it helped Alan to consider where his style had come from. On the few occasions when he had behaved aggressively in his childhood he had been harshly punished. As one of the smallest children in his grade at school, he had been pushed around a lot. His rage combined with a fear of being attacked had led him to find a way of expressing both at once. He had become a very funny satirist, the class clown, and had been adept at manipulating the world from behind the scenes. He saw the reasons for his behavior, and he began to see its effects as well.

For Alan, overcoming the passive-aggressive style meant both becoming assertive and, oddly enough, giving up. He practiced assertiveness skills in safe situations, despite deep misgivings about their likely effectiveness. His dissatisfaction with his life enabled him to push past his reluctance, however. He began being assertive in minor situations: requesting supplies, discussing small issues with supervisors, communicating clearly with coworkers. Despite some unsatisfying outcomes, he had enough successes to keep going. He began to feel more relaxed around work.

Giving up meant playing a less central role in office politics and not trying to control others. He withdrew from several committees and identified certain issues about which he would not gossip. Gradually, some of these issues began to seem less important to him. For a while he feared that he was "losing his edge," but his job performance was improving. He tried refusing tasks that he knew he would never complete, and he attempted to fulfill the obligations he accepted. Despite improvements, he realized that he was not really suited to a large government office and began to contemplate a career change.

It was more difficult for Alan to practice assertiveness skills in social situations, since he had virtually no social life. He joined a local hiking group. This gave him the opportunity to socialize along the trail. He tried to keep himself from speaking about anyone in the group behind their back. His sense of humor was a major point in his favor, but he labored to keep from using it as a weapon. He began to feel less isolated. By the end of therapy he had several friends and was preparing to begin dating again. Light had appeared in the tunnel.

Checkpoint: A Self-Assessment

Take some time now to explore your reasons for holding this book in your hands. Based on what you already know about assertiveness, what do you think of your own abilities?

Make a mark on the line below to indicate where you think you are now.

Not very good.   So-so.   Great.
Much less assertive   About as assertive   More assertive
than most people.   as most people.   than most people.

Where do you hope to be when you finish this workbook? Mark the line with an X.

_____

Briefly list three situations in your life in which you would like to be more assertive.

1. _____

_____

_____

2. _____

_____

_____

3. _____

_____

_____

Now take some time to complete the following sentences:

I get most passive when _____

_____

_____

I often become aggressive when _____

_____

_____

My biggest fear of being assertive is _____

_____

_____

The two people in my life that I find it hardest to be assertive with are _____

_____

_____

I am already quite assertive when _____

_____

_____

    Keep these answers in mind as you consider the barriers to assertive behavior covered in the next three chapters.

CHAPTER 2

OVERCOMING THE
STRESS BARRIER

Perhaps you are already convinced that the assertive style usually works better than being passive, aggressive, or passive-aggressive. Why doesn't everyone use it, then? One reason is that it involves a series of very specific skills, which are covered in Part Two of this book. The other reason is that a variety of barriers hold people back. One of these barriers is housed within your body: the stress response. Overcoming the stress barrier requires an understanding of the nature of stress and of the ways you manage it.

What Is Stress?

In brief, the stress response is a bodily reaction to the perception that we are under threat. It's as simple as that.

If you have allergies, you probably know that the allergy symptoms are not really produced by the peanuts, the bee sting, the pollen, the dust, or the dog dander. The things that you are allergic to are not, in themselves, dangerous. The problem lies in your immune system. Your body detects the allergen, misinterprets it as something dangerous, and mounts an enormous immune reaction designed to overcome the danger. In some cases (such as some peanut allergies), this "helper" response can actually endanger the person's life. It is the body's response that produces the symptoms, not the thing to which you are allergic. Most treatments for allergies are designed to calm the immune system; to relax its attempts to "help" you.

Stress is similar. It feels as though it is produced by traffic, demanding family members, your job, your parachuting instructor, and so on. But it isn't. Stress is produced by your body. This is why it is called the stress *response*. It is designed to help you cope with these stressful situations.

But there is a problem. Most people feel *less* able to cope when the stress response is activated. How does this "helper" response wind up doing more harm than good?

The answer is that the stress response developed at a time when the biggest threats to well-being involved violent life-or-death conflict. A predator might appear on the scene. You might be attacked by a neighboring group or tribe. To get food you might have to go on the attack yourself. In situations like these, the best odds for survival usually involve one of two options:

1. Fight as hard as you can.

2. Run away as fast as you can.

Survival may depend on how hard you fight or how fast you run. Those who fight the hardest or run the fastest are more likely to live and, therefore, to pass along their characteristics to their children. The result is an environmental pressure favoring those who 1) are strong and 2) can make the most of the muscles they have in an emergency.

It would be nice to be able to say to a saber-toothed tiger, *"You just wait right here and I'll go to the gym for a few months to bulk up; then I'll come back and deal with you."* Unfortunately, this isn't practical. Instead, the body developed the stress response: a system of reorganizing the normal functions of the body to give top priority to running and fighting. This is why it is also called the "fight or flight response." The trigger for the stress response to be activated is a perception that we are under threat.

When the stress response is triggered, a host of changes take place in our bodies. These include:

- An increase in heart rate to pump blood more quickly to working muscles.

- An increase in pulse volume—the amount of blood the heart pumps with every beat (this is responsible for the feeling of your heart pounding in your chest).

- Increased respiration to ensure the availability of oxygen to burn energy.

- A rise in blood sugar via the release of glucose from the liver (to fuel the muscles).

- Increased blood supply to the large muscles through vasodilation, the widening of blood vessels in these muscles.

- Decreased blood supply to the skin and the digestive system via vasoconstriction, the narrowing of blood vessels in these areas.

- The release of endorphins (natural painkillers) to prevent us from being disabled or slowed down by the pain of injury (though with extended stress, pain sensitivity actually rises).

- A host of other physical changes.

The stress response causes psychological and behavioral changes as well. The senses become more acute. Time may seem to slow down. You become more able to focus on specific vital tasks (like running or fighting) and, correspondingly, less able to focus on multiple complex tasks. Creative thinking declines. A desire to move takes over, often resulting in pacing, fidgeting, or an intense sense of restlessness. Certain emotions are intensified. If you believe the situation is beyond your control, you are likely to experience fear. You may feel a desire to escape. If it appears that attacking might help, you may feel anger instead.

In sum, you become stronger, faster, more focused, and more resistant to pain when the stress response is activated. If you find yourself in a situation in which you have to run or fight, the stress response is likely to help. Sometime in your life the stress response is likely to save you from harm.

But all of these changes were designed to help you out in primitive environments. You no longer live in such an environment (even though some days it may seem otherwise). The kinds of pressures that you experience in the modern world are not usually helped by attack or escape. Indeed, these responses make most of the situations you face worse, not better.

Take a moment to think about the kinds of pressures you really face on a regular basis.

Write down one of the situations in which you felt yourself becoming stressed in the past week.

_____

_____

Would running away and screaming really have helped you to cope with this situation?

_____

Can you remember *wanting* to escape the situation?

_____

Would physically attacking someone really have helped?

_____

Can you remember *wanting* to attack someone (strike your child, smack your boss, shove your partner)?

_____

If attack or escape really are your best options, then the stress response is likely to help. If not, then it will do more harm than good. It may seem at the time as though running away from our children or striking the boss is a good idea, but ultimately it will make things worse. Instead, we may need to do what we do with allergies: calm down the "helper" response.

How do we turn off (or turn down) the stress response? To answer that question we need to be a bit more explicit about the nature of stress. Here's the idea:

Situation   ⇨   *Appraisal*   ⇨   *Response*

Stress-Related Resistance

Stress is typically triggered by an event in the outside world. The boss frowns, your child starts screaming in the grocery store, the car fails to start, or a friend doesn't show up as planned. None of these situations alone will produce the stress response. They must first be perceived and appraised. If you don't notice the boss frowning, you won't feel anything. Furthermore, the appraisal must indicate that you are being threatened somehow. If you think the frown comes from eating too much at lunch, you probably won't worry. If you think it means she's about to fire you, a stress response is likely to result.

Underlying the whole process is your own bodily resistance to stress. Some people just react more readily than others. You probably know someone who seldom seems to get anxious or upset, no matter what happens. People vary in how easily their stress response is triggered. Some of this difference is probably inborn. There is evidence that some babies are more easily stressed than others, and these differences appear to last into adulthood. But some aspects of stress-related resistance are due to lifestyle factors.

You can cope with stress at any stage in the process:

- You can deal with the situation itself (for example, by confronting the person responsible). This is the point of most assertiveness strategies. If your stress response is too active, however, you may find it hard to use assertive techniques.

- You can re-evaluate your appraisal. Perhaps you are making too much of the situation. Does the frown necessarily mean you are about to be fired? Are you really that bad of an employee? If your new appraisal is less threatening than the old one, the stress response is likely to subside.

- You can deal with the bodily response itself by engaging in relaxation techniques.

- If you become stressed too easily, you can make some lifestyle changes that will increase your resistance to stress.

Before getting into the specifics of these techniques, let's examine how the stress response affects assertive behavior.

Stress and Assertiveness

As we have discussed, most of the pressures we face in the modern world are very different from those in the primitive world. Running away usually doesn't help very much. Neither does attacking people physically. Most of the time, these choices only make things worse.

Instead, the best thing to do is usually to stay calm, think through your options, decide on a course of action, and then carry it out. To be *assertive* we have to think about the words we are using and express ourselves without either shrinking away or becoming aggressive. This is precisely what the stress response *prevents* us from doing well.

Take a look at the diagram below. Imagine a situation: A coworker criticizes some work you have done. Your reaction will depend on what you think this *means*. If you believe that your job depends on how well you do this task, you may see the criticism as a threat. This is your *appraisal*.

Once you feel threatened you will probably show signs of the stress response. This includes some or all of the physical changes discussed above (rapid heart rate and so on), plus changes in the way you think.

Stress and Unassertive Behavior

Situation
⇩
Appraisal of Threat
⇩
Stress Response
⇩

Fear	Fear and Anger	Anger
⇩	⇩	⇩
Flight Response	Combined Response	Fight Response
⇩	⇩	⇩
Desire to Avoid Conflict	Desire to Win AND Avoid Conflict	Desire to Win
⇩	⇩	⇩
Passive Behavior	Passive-Aggressive Behavior	Aggressive Behavior

---

If you believe that you are likely to lose your job, you may become frightened. Fear activates the flight response (the desire to escape). You will probably want to avoid the situation and any conflict that it brings. As a result, you may find yourself behaving in a passive manner. Perhaps you will mutter something to your coworker and remove yourself from the situation as soon as possible.

If instead you believe that your coworker is wrong and that you don't deserve the criticism, then you may become angry. This brings on the "fight" side of the stress response. You may want to win out over your coworker. As a result, you may become aggressive. Perhaps you will begin speaking in a loud and threatening voice about your coworker's own shortcomings.

A third possibility is that you will become angry but still fear a direct confrontation. Your response may be a mix of the passive and aggressive styles. Perhaps you will avoid the coworker but begin whispering about their faults to others. Or you may do something to make their own work look bad. This would be classic passive-aggressive behavior.

All three of these responses (passive, aggressive, and passive-aggressive) will probably make the situation worse in the long run. The alternative is to engage in assertive behavior. But to do so, you may have to calm the stress response. How do we do this?

Building Stress-Related Resistance

One strategy for calming the stress response is to increase your physical resistance to stress. Some people find that their body is on a hair-trigger: Almost any challenge will activate the stress response. If this is the case, it can be helpful for you to consider changing your lifestyle. Certain changes may make you less vulnerable to stress.

Think about your own vulnerability to stress compared to the people you know. In general, do you become stressed more easily or less easily than others? Estimate by marking the line below:

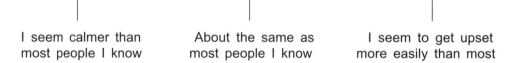

I seem calmer than   About the same as   I seem to get upset
most people I know   most people I know   more easily than most

If you marked the line to the right of the midpoint or if you would like to manage stress even better, you might wish to consider some of the following strategies. Place a checkmark beside those ideas that seem most appropriate for your own life.

☐ **Exercise**. Research indicates that people who engage in regular exercise tend to exhibit less stress and anxiety than those who don't (Hays 1999). It does not seem to matter whether the activity is aerobic or anaerobic; what's important is the participation in regular fitness activities. Pick a variety of activities that you enjoy (or at least can tolerate), remember to stretch and warm up each time, and do them regularly (three to four times a week is best). Don't overdo it, and ask your physician's advice before starting a new or strenuous fitness regimen. The benefits typically begin to develop quite quickly, often within three to four weeks.

☐ **Eat well**. Eating irregular meals of greasy, unhealthy food while on the run appears to contribute to a vulnerability to stress. Regular, nutritionally balanced meals are a better option. These do not have to be elaborate, multicourse feasts that require hours to plan and cook. Relatively simple measures, such as choosing salads over french fries or taking the time to sit down and eat calmly, can be extremely helpful. Some people find that the simple sugars found in sweets cause roller-coaster changes in mood ranging from speediness to lethargy; complex carbohydrates may be a better option. Consult your physician for guidelines on proper eating and nutrition, or get a copy of the USDA's *Food Pyramid* or Health and Welfare Canada's *Canada Food Guide*. Both can be obtained through government offices or from the Internet (simply search using the titles).

☐ **Get enough sleep**. Lots of people don't get enough sleep, and sleep deprivation is a clear contributor to vulnerability to stress. Make getting a good night's sleep a high priority in your life. Most people need between seven and nine hours of sleep each night for best performance, though there are wide individual differences. For best results, maintain a regular bedtime and rising time. The body's twenty-four-hour sleep/wake cycle can be easily disrupted by changes in these times over the course of your week. Ensure that your sleeping environment is conducive to sleep in terms of temperature, quiet, and darkness. If you have difficulty sleeping, consult your physician. You may also find it helpful to consult a book on sleep problems, such as *Getting to Sleep* (Catalano 1990).

☐ **Watch your caffeine intake**. Caffeine is an addictive substance that chemically stimulates the stress response system. The primary sources of caffeine are coffee (about 200 mg per 8 oz. cup), tea (about 70 mg per cup), caffeinated soft drinks (30-60 mg per cup), and chocolate (about 25 mg in a small bar). If anxiety, fear, and/or anger are significant difficulties for you or if you have trouble sleeping, it is probably best for you to moderate your caffeine intake. If you consume more than about 450 mg per day (depending on your body weight and other factors), sudden withdrawal could very well result in headaches, irritability, and difficulty concentrating. To avoid these reactions, reduce your intake gradually. Although caffeine and its effects are not themselves dangerous for most people, excessive intake can play a significant role in stress-related problems.

☐ **Lead a balanced life**. Do you work sixteen hours a day? Do you try to juggle too many tasks? Do you often find yourself multitasking (talking on the phone while eating, watching television, ironing, and filling out your income tax form all at the same time)? If so, then stress management may not be the problem. Your life is the problem. You may be leading a life that naturally and predictably causes you to feel chronically stressed. As a result, you will find yourself being pulled toward passive, aggressive, and/or passive-aggressive behavior. Furthermore, you probably aren't having much fun. Although you may still learn a great deal from the skills in this workbook, you may need seriously to consider cutting back in some areas of your life. Remember: No one ever reaches the end of life and says, *"I wish I'd spent more time at the office."*

This is not by any means an exhaustive list of strategies to increase stress-related resistance. For more ideas, you may wish to consult an excellent book by Edmund Bourne (1998) entitled *Healing Fear*.

Examining Your Appraisals

A second strategy for dealing with stress is to examine the way you are thinking about the situation at hand. This corresponds to the "appraisal" stage in the diagram a few pages back. Sometimes we misinterpret situations as being more threatening than they really are.

In order to relate this idea to your own life, think of a stressful situation that has happened in the past week or two. Ideally, it should be a relatively minor event that produced a big reaction in you. What was the situation?

_____

_____

Cognitive-behavioral theory suggests that we don't really react to what's going on around us. Instead, we react to what we *think* is going on. Sometimes we're right. Sometimes we're wrong. This isn't a new idea. Epictetus (A.D. 50-135) said, *"People are disturbed not by things, but by the views which they take of them."*

Now, if you reacted in a big emotional way to a relatively small event, perhaps it wasn't really the event that brought about the reaction. Instead, it was what the event *meant* to you. Perhaps it wasn't so much that your friend was late for lunch but that you decided it meant she doesn't really respect you. Your emotional reaction isn't to her lateness but to not being respected.

Appraisals about what situations really mean commonly take place automatically, often without our awareness. We become upset and sometimes we don't know why. The trick is to ask ourselves what we think the situation *meant*, to evaluate that meaning, and to substitute a different meaning, if we think we were being unrealistic.

Think about the stressful situation you previously identified. What did it mean to you that this situation occurred? What did it tell you about yourself, or the other person, or the world, or the past, or the future?

_____

_____

_____

Are you 100 percent certain that the situation really means what you thought it meant? Or only 98 percent certain? Or less? Or, now that you look at it, did it not really mean what you thought at all?

_____

Take another look at the situation. Examine it from another point of view. Are there other possible explanations? What are they?

_____

_____

_____

_____

Are the alternative explanations you've identified as threatening as the one you first came up with? Perhaps they are even worse. Often, however, they are not quite as bad. Stress doesn't just *result* from overly negative appraisals. Stress can also *produce* them. When we are tense, for whatever reason, we tend to come up with more negative or catastrophic interpretations of events. And we tend to be more certain of our interpretations than is warranted.

Here are some strategies for questioning and altering appraisals. Place a checkmark beside those that you would like to practice.

☐ **Is my life in danger?** Remember that the stress response is designed to save your life. Most of the time when we become tense, our lives are not in any danger. The stress response is being activated completely needlessly. *"Yes, I only have an hour and I don't know what to buy James for his birthday. But it's not a life-threatening situation."* The strategy? Simply ask yourself, *"Is my life in danger?"* Then answer the question. Once you realize that you are safe, that you aren't really being seriously threatened, you may be able to let go of some of the tension.

☐ **Will being tense help the situation?** It sometimes feels very important to be tense. The situation seems perilous to us and it feels as though we *should* be tense. But the tension is really only good for two things: fighting and running. Are either of those responses likely to be a big help? If not, then perhaps you can let go of some of the tension. *"No, I guess holding onto the steering wheel with a vise grip isn't going to get me there any faster. I can lighten up a little."*

☐ **What is the worst thing that could happen?** We often have a feeling of great tension associated with relatively minor events. It can be worthwhile to ask yourself this question and think about the worst possible outcome. If your feared outcome were to happen, could you live with it? If so, then you don't really *need* the situation to work out the way you want it to. You'd *prefer* it, but you don't need it. *"Even if he yells at me for not completing the project, I'll survive. I can allow for that possibility."*

☐ **Do a three-column form.** Cognitive therapists often use column-style forms as a way of exploring alternative ways of thinking. The simplest is the three-column form, reproduced on the next page.

In the first column you write down the situation. In the second, you say how you immediately interpreted the situation. These "automatic thoughts" are often distorted or extreme. In the third column you say what you logically believe to be true and raise other possible interpretations. In the process of writing a three-column form you will often realize that you were assuming you knew what was going on when you didn't and that your assumptions may have been overly negative. This can help to reduce stress because you find that you aren't being threatened after all or that the threat is more minor than you had thought.

Situation	Automatic Thoughts	The Truth
Frank asked me to serve on the office space allocation committee.	He'll hate me if I say no.	He's entitled to feel what he feels; besides, he probably won't hate me.
	I'm not allowed to say no.	I decide what I will and won't do. I'm not trapped into doing anything.
	He knows what an awful job it is; he asked because he hates me.	He's done other things that suggest he likes me. Maybe he thinks it's an honor. Maybe he's already tried everyone else.
	He has no idea how much work I've already done.	Maybe he does know and thinks he can rely on me to do it well. If I want him to know about my work, it's up to me to tell him.

Most of us have long-standing beliefs about ourselves, about assertiveness, and about social expectations that have an impact on the way we think in challenging interpersonal situations. It can be immensely helpful to know what these are and to catch them at work. These beliefs are the subject of chapter 4.

Calming the Stress Response

Another way of handling tension is to calm the stress response directly. Entire books have been written on this subject, and you may wish to consult additional sources to develop effective relaxation skills. *The Relaxation and Stress Reduction Workbook* (Davis, Eschelman, and McKay 2000) is an excellent example. Here we will consider only three options, though there are many more.

1. **Insert a gap**. If you're already tense it will take some time for you to regain some perspective. Getting away from the trigger situation for a while will often help you to regain the upper hand over the stress response. Go for a walk, take a break on your own, spend some time on an unrelated task, meditate—whatever it takes. If necessary, a washroom cubicle will give you some space to yourself. If you absolutely cannot leave the situation, then ensure that you leave a gap before you

respond. Stress tends to make us more impulsive; we say the first thing that comes to us. Given the way that stress works, your first response is likely to be too passive or too aggressive (or both). The old strategy of counting to ten before answering sometimes works: it gives you time to think of an alternate, assertive response. If you have been criticized, you can see if there is any truth in it. You may have to ask for clarification. Then you can work on a response that acknowledges what has been said without either avoiding or attacking.

2. **Burn it off**. The stress response prepares you to engage in vigorous physical activity. If you just sit there, the physical symptoms (and the behavioral tendencies accompanying them) will take time to pass. An alternative is to do exactly what the response intends you to do: exercise. A run, a swim, a squash game, a brisk walk—all of these can help burn off the nervous energy that the stress response brings, leaving you calmer and more able to deal with the situation assertively. One caution, though: If you exercise when you are tense and impulsive, you are more likely to overdo it and, possibly, suffer a sports-related injury. Remember to stretch and warm up first, and refrain from overexertion.

3. **Breathe**. When we become tense we tend to breathe more shallowly and rapidly. Our chest muscles work more and our diaphragm works less. Some people find that they hold their breath when they're stressed. These changes in breathing can bring on many of the physical symptoms of stress: light-headedness, tingling sensations in the hands and feet, dizziness, and a feeling of constriction in the chest. Consequently, it is a good idea to use stress, anxiety, or anger as a cue to engage in deliberate, slow, diaphragmatic breathing. A diaphragmatic breathing exercise is described below. Don't wait until you feel anxious to try it out, though. It takes plenty of practice before you can use it successfully to combat stress on the spot.

A Quick Breathing Exercise

We breathe using two sets of muscles. One set pulls the ribs forward (making the chest appear bigger). The other set lowers the diaphragm (a sheet of tissue separating the chest from the abdomen). This makes your stomach stick out when you inhale.

The following breathing exercise uses both sets of muscles. To do the exercise you may find it helpful to imagine that you actually have two sets of lungs: one set in your chest and the other in your stomach. If you have asthma or other breathing difficulties, please consult your physician before trying this exercise.

First, place one hand on your abdomen and the other hand on your upper chest. Then proceed through these four steps:

1. Breathe in deeply using your diaphragm. Your stomach should expand and your chest should remain still. Imagine that the lungs in your stomach (which feel like they exist, even though they don't) are inflating, while your chest lungs remain inactive.

2. Without breathing out, breathe in further—this time using the muscles of your chest. Your chest should expand (moving forward and slightly up) while your stomach remains inflated.

3. Breathe out slowly and naturally. Don't push or blow the air out. Simply relax and let go. Exhaling should be completely passive; allow the air to go without forcing it out.

4. Pause for a few seconds before starting the whole process over again. Because you are inhaling more air with each breath, you will need to breathe at a much slower pace than usual.

Repeat the procedure for at least five breaths. Some people notice a sensation of dizziness or tingling as they do this type of breathing. This means that they are breathing too quickly. Use these sensations as cues to slow down your breathing. Just lengthen all four of the steps.

Practice the exercise twice a day for several minutes each time. Keep this up until you can do it without having your hands in place and while you are walking. At that point, you may be ready to begin using the technique in stressful situations to relax yourself.

We've covered coping with stress by working with bodily resistance (your lifestyle), with your appraisals, and with the stress response itself. Isn't there something else? Of course: dealing with the situation itself. That's what Part Two of this book is all about. But before you try to deal with the situation, you may need to deal with your stress response.

Which of the techniques listed in the last few pages do you need to work on the most? Find two. (Hint: Diaphragmatic breathing should be one of them for almost everyone.)

1. _____

2. _____

Come up with a plan for implementing these changes.

For No. 1:

_____

_____

_____

For No. 2:

_____

_____

_____

Return to this page in a week or two and record any progress you've made and/or challenges you've encountered.

Life gets simpler as it goes along. As you deal with the stress response more effectively, you will discover that you are pulled less and less into nonassertive behavior. As well, the stress response interferes more drastically with skills that you are just learning than with well-learned skills. As you practice the assertiveness skills in Part Two of this manual, they will tend to become more automatic. As they do, you will find that it becomes easier and easier to be assertive when you are under pressure.

CHAPTER 3

OVERCOMING THE SOCIAL BARRIER

Assertiveness is meant to improve our interpersonal relationships. As a result, we might expect everyone around us to be very enthusiastic when we become more assertive. We might imagine that they will be extremely encouraging and supportive.

Well, don't count on it. In fact, the reverse is often true. The people around you may resist your efforts to become more assertive—even if it will help your relationships with them in the long run. Certain people in your social circle will try to push you back into your old way of relating, even if they used to complain about it. The closer the relationship, the more you may find that assertiveness strategies cause disturbances. This is especially likely if your usual style has been passive—though it also happens to those who are more used to being aggressive or passive-aggressive.

Why aren't people more supportive of the change? There are several reasons.

The "What Does This Mean?" Problem

The people in your life have become accustomed to your style of communicating. If you are usually aggressive, they have come to expect you to be aggressive. If you are usually passive, they expect you to be passive. If you are usually passive-aggressive, they come to expect that from you. They may not *like* any of these styles. They may see your current style as a barrier to the relationship and to developing greater closeness with you. And they may well be right. They may even have been telling you that they'd like you to change your style. *"Please, please, tell me what you'd like for once!"*

But many people fear change. No matter how many holes an old sweater has, it is still familiar. Imagine how odd it would be to find that suddenly your old sweater didn't have holes anymore. You might wonder what had happened. Did someone mend it? Is this really your sweater? Did someone switch it on you? Are you losing your mind?

When you change your way of relating to others, they will wonder what's going on. Why have you changed? What does it mean? Do you still like them? Do you still need them? Are you angry? Are you depressed? Are you planning something behind their backs? Are you the same person they've always known? What's going to happen to the relationship? Any change in style, even a welcome one, can be alarming to the people close to you. It signals that other things may need to change as well.

As a result, you may notice some of the people in your life becoming anxious as you become more assertive. They may ask *"What's wrong?"* or say, *"You're not yourself today."* It will take time for them to realize that you are still the same person but that you are becoming more open and honest. It can be a good idea to tell them that you are trying to change your style, and why. *"I'm trying to speak up about things a little more than I used to do. That way I don't get resentful and everyone doesn't have to guess what I really think."*

Are there people in your life who might be alarmed if you suddenly became assertive? Who? Name two. For each one, make a note of which style of communication they are used to you using. Then see if you can come up with a relaxed, casual way of letting them know that you're thinking of changing your style. Ask them for support if you like. Above all, be brief and casual. You aren't becoming a completely different person, after all, and the change isn't going to be all that sudden. This is a project, not a revolution.

1. Name of person _____ Style they expect: _____

What could you say? _____

_____

_____

2. Name of person _____ Style they expect: _____

What could you say? _____

_____

_____

Now: Think carefully. Could you handle it if one or both of these people aren't supportive? They might not be, and you have to allow for that possibility. Are you willing to *allow* them not to be supportive? If so, then consider whether or not to actually tell them. Once you've tried it with one person, consider whether to try it out on others.

The History Problem

Your friends and family have learned to interpret your behavior. They know how assertive you usually are, and they know what is unusual *for you*. If you usually behave passively, for example, they may know that you only speak your mind when you feel very strongly. As a result, when you become assertive, they may overinterpret your behavior. *"That would be normal conversation for anyone else, but coming from you it must mean you're furious!"* Even if you manage to be assertive in a relaxed, friendly way, they may think it means you are a volcano about to erupt.

They may also misinterpret your attempts to be assertive if you have usually been aggressive. Your friends may be used to you yelling and pounding your fist when you mean what you say. If you adopt a more pleasant and relaxed assertive style, they may not realize that you are serious at first. With time, they will learn that you mean what you say even if you aren't yelling.

If you have been passive-aggressive, they may wonder what it means when you speak openly and plainly. Are you enraged? Do you mean it? Are you being sarcastic? Is there a trick? Keep at it and they'll learn.

Recognize that this barrier is not necessarily the fault of the people around you. They are not being mean or inconsiderate. It is simply that you are not behaving according to their expectations. Who established those expectations? Well . . . you did. By behaving passively, aggressively, or passive-aggressively, you have encouraged people to expect that style from you. This isn't meant to make you feel guilty. After all, there are reasons why you have adopted the style you have. But it may not be appropriate to blame your friends for expecting more of the same from you.

Key Point: Don't blame others for expecting passivity or aggression from you—especially if you were the one to create those expectations.

Who in your life might be confused when you begin to behave assertively?

_____

_____

What could you say if they don't understand? One option will be to go back to your old style (get enraged, get passive, get even). Are you willing to stay assertive and give them time to adjust? What are your thoughts about this?

_____

_____

_____

The Control Problem

When you behave passively, control of your life is in the hands of the people around you. They can do anything in the relationship and you will not object. They can ask you to do anything and you will do it. They get their way. This is a tremendous amount of power that you give them.

People like to be powerful and in control. It helps us to feel secure. If I can control you, then I have a helper to assist me whenever I want one. This is tremendously convenient. Even though I may not believe in controlling others, I can probably explain away any guilt that it brings. *"You were bored and needed something to do, so I gave you an errand." "You like to feel needed." "You enjoy doing my dirty work."* Naturally enough, I may resist if you try to take that control back. No one likes to lose power.

When you become more assertive, you begin taking control of your own life. Obviously, this means taking control back from the people you have given it to. They will resist. Count on it. Remember, though, that the control was never really in their hands. You had it all along. But now you are exercising it.

Key Point: Expect resistance when you assume control over your own life.

Caution: If someone in your life has a history of violence toward you, they may feel accustomed to having control. If you take control back, they may feel threatened and they might engage in more violence. Seek additional help or counseling to deal with these situations.

Have you given control of parts of your life to other people? Who?

_____

How might they react when you start taking back the reins of your life?

_____

_____

_____

Are you prepared to handle these reactions? How? Are you able to have compassion for them if they feel they are losing the control you have given them in the past?

_____

_____

_____

The Boundary-Setting Problem

People are used to having a certain amount of freedom. Assertiveness often involves setting boundaries around what you will and will not tolerate—

especially when it affects you. Whenever you put up a personal boundary, others will usually struggle against it.

Key Point: When you start being assertive with someone, things usually get worse before they get better.

Imagine that you live in a cooperative housing complex. One of the other residents constantly has you do some of her chores. One day you tell her that you have enough to do and that from now on you won't do her work. What happens? She will probably try to push her work onto you even harder than she did before.

Giving in under this pressure is a bad idea. In effect, you would be saying, *"Look, if I ever tell you what I will or won't do, act really pushy and I'll give in."* This is a bad message. If, instead, you stick to your new rule of assertiveness, she will eventually give up and stop pushing.

Here's another example: You have a child who insists on staying up watching television after her bedtime. You become assertive and tell her, *"If you are not in bed by your bedtime, I will turn the television off and you will not be able to watch TV the next night."* At first your daughter may not believe you and may respond with outrage if you follow through on your promise. If you are able to keep to this new plan, however, she will eventually adapt to the new rule and abide by it.

Here are some guidelines:

- **Only set boundaries that you are willing and able to defend**. If you make threats that you cannot keep (*"I'll quit this job, leave you, ground you for a year, never speak to you again, etc."*), people will not take your attempts to be assertive seriously.

- **Don't start getting assertive when you are strained to the limit**. Remember that the relationship will get even tougher for a while. Pick a time when you have the strength to handle the pressure.

- **Don't back down**. When you set the barrier in place and the other person begins pushing against it, be prepared to keep to the rule. Otherwise, they will push harder the next time.

- **Don't become assertive with everyone in your life at once**. You probably won't be able to stand having all of your relationships becoming more difficult at once. Pick one person at a time.

Now take some time to think about your own social network (including spouse, children, other family, friends, and coworkers). If you become more assertive in your relationships, who is likely to resist the change? Keep in mind that they may do so because they don't know what your behavior means, because they expect you to behave a certain way based on your history, or because they like the control your present style gives them.

List the names of these people.

_____

_____

Now, go back over the list and rate how difficult you think each person will be in accepting and adapting to your more assertive style of communication. Use a 0–10 scale, where 0 means "no problem" and 10 means "total resistance."

Remember, you won't suddenly be assertive with everyone at once. You can use your ratings to help you decide whom to choose first. In general, it is a good idea to start with people you think will react reasonably well. Prepare yourself, though. Sometimes you will be surprised.

The Gender Problem

Your gender can result in a number of barriers to being assertive. You may have ideas and expectations about how a man or woman behaves. The people who raised you had expectations based on gender, and some of these they taught to you. The people you meet on a day-to-day basis have their own expectations, which you may or may not be willing to live up to. Gender-based ideas and expectations can create barriers whether you are male or female.

Barriers to Being an Assertive Woman

Women often find that the barriers are particularly demanding, widely held, and difficult to leap over. Most of these barriers enforce a passive manner of responding. Let's first consider some of the barriers that most commonly plague women. Place a checkmark beside any that apply especially to you. If you are a man, read them anyway; many men are raised with these barriers as well.

☐ **You were raised to serve others**. If you experience this barrier, you received the message that your job is to support others in their lives rather than live your own. Rather than resulting in a healthy balance between living one's own life and supporting others (a good idea), this leads to tremendous guilt at doing anything just for yourself. Because your guidance for your life comes almost entirely from the demands of others, you may have difficulty even *knowing* what you would like, let alone doing it.

☐ **You were raised to be nice**. Your job is to be polite. Not a bad goal in itself, but here the definition of "nice" means never to say "no," never to disagree, never to have a boundary between you and others, and never to reveal your own desires or opinions.

☐ **Your relationship is your worth**. Without a romantic relationship, you are nothing. As a result, you can never run the risk of damaging a relationship by raising your own needs, wants, opinions, or personality—in other words, by actually being there. This belief may come from upbringing, peers, or the media or culture at large.

☐ **You are the family maid (or butler)**. Members of your family believe that childcare, housekeeping, cooking, and more are solely your responsibility—not because you agreed to this or because you have the time, but because of your gender. Women who work identical hours to their mates often find that they are still expected to take the lead at home.

☐ **You are the old family retainer**. In family situations, women are often expected to take a more active caretaking role. Brothers, for example, may assume that their sisters will take the lead in caring for aging parents.

☐ **You are the junior partner**. Your partner (or others) expects you to be more passive and agreeable than you would like. As a result, you are the one who always gives in, and your partner is the one who makes all the big decisions (and most of the little ones). There may even be a threat of violence if you try to take a more active role.

☐ **You are the junior employee (even if you're not)**. At work you may find that supervisors expect the women to do more menial tasks or to be easier to "push around" than the men. *"Just type this up, please, Elizabeth—I mean Mrs. Dole . . . ."* You may need to be more assertive than the men at your workplace because the men may not have to deal with as many unreasonable requests. (This is not true everywhere, obviously, but it is far from uncommon.)

☐ **You're not as important as a man**. This means that in public settings you have noticed that you do not receive the same courtesy as men. You may be less likely to obtain a loan, you may have more difficulty receiving adequate service, or people may behave in a condescending manner that seems related to your gender.

This is far from an exhaustive list. If you are a woman, perhaps you have noticed other barriers to being assertive based on your gender. See if you can think of at least one more that has affected your life. What is it?

_____

_____

_____

_____

Barriers to Being an Assertive Man

Men, too, may find themselves pulled away from assertive responses based on gender expectations. Some of these pull toward aggressive behavior, while others pull toward passive or passive-aggressive behavior. Place a checkmark beside those that seem to fit your life. If you are a woman, you may find some of these also apply to you.

☐ **A man is a man**. You were raised to believe that real men are aggressive and pushy, demanding rather than asking for what they want. Your job is to be in control of others as well as yourself. It's a sign of weakness to let others do what they want. As a result, you have adopted an aggressive stance.

☐ **Obey, or else**. Some men were raised by demanding, overpowering authority figures who expected passive obedience. Any attempt to be assertive was viewed by the authority figure (often the father) as a challenge to his rule and was vigorously struck down. The result can be a fear of being assertive, coupled with a feeling of being an imposter when you stand up for yourself. *"What if they see through me?"*

☐ **A man has no self**. The role of a man is to be the breadwinner and selfless warrior on behalf of others. He is to have no personal interests, he needs no breaks, and he requires no nurturing. He is a rock, emotionless and solid. As a result, he can't ask for help, he can't share emotion, and he can't speak of his own needs.

☐ **A man can take it**. Being overwhelmed by work is a sign of weakness. Conversely, taking on a heavier load than anyone else is a source of pride. The consequence is an inability to say no, resulting in an unreasonable workload and the risk of burnout or exhaustion.

This list, too, is incomplete. If you are a man, try to think of gender-based expectations (your own or those of others) that have held you back from behaving assertively (and may have resulted in aggressive, passive, or passive-aggressive behavior). Write these down.

Considerations for Both Men and Women

Whether you are male or female, do you believe that you were raised to be passive, aggressive, or passive-aggressive based on your gender? If so, which style was most encouraged?

During your upbringing, who encouraged you to adopt a nonassertive style? Why?

Think about your present life. Are there situations now in which assertiveness is discouraged (or one of the nonassertive styles is encouraged) by virtue of your being male or female? Which situations are those?

_____

_____

_____

Do you still believe that it is important that you *not* be assertive? If so, what are your reasons?

_____

_____

_____

There are no easy solutions to these problems faced by men and women. One of the most important tasks is to become aware of the beliefs and fears about assertiveness that can be based on gender. More beliefs that prevent us from being assertive are discussed in the next chapter.

CHAPTER 4

OVERCOMING THE BELIEF
BARRIER

Do you live in the real world? The temptation is probably to answer "yes." Cognitive therapists believe, however, that the correct answer is "no." An explanation is clearly in order.

It seems as though we see the world the way it really is, and we react to it predictably. Something good happens, for instance, and we react positively. Something bad happens and we react negatively. Our reactions include our behavior, emotions, and some physical changes, such as smiling, flushing, shaking, relaxing, tensing, and so on. In other words:

Situation in the Real World   ⇨   *Reaction*

As we discussed in chapter 2, however, this model is not accurate. We don't really react to what is going on in the real world; we react to what we *think* is going on. Our behavior and emotions depend more on our *interpretation* of events than on the events themselves. If the patron ahead of us in a bank lineup reaches into his pocket, we interpret what his behavior means. If we think he is reaching for his wallet, we don't react much. If we think he is reaching for a gun, we may start to sweat. The physical act of reaching does not produce our reaction. Instead, we react to our idea of what the action means. We live in a world of beliefs and ideas. Our thoughts are influenced by what happens in the real world, but our interpretations produce most of our reactions.

Where do the interpretations come from? There are two primary influences. The first is the perception of the event itself. If a runaway car is headed your way but you don't see it, you won't react. If you do see it, you will react strongly. The second, and crucial, influence on the appraisal is your system of beliefs about yourself, about other people, and about the world and how it works.

Here, then, is a better version of the diagram above:

Situation   ⇨   **Appraisal**   ⇨   **Response**

⇧

Beliefs

The three items in a line across the top resemble elements in the diagram you saw in chapter 2. We have simply added the influence of "Beliefs" to clarify their role in the appraisal process. An event happens in the real world. You interpret your perception of that event based on your beliefs about how the world works. And you react accordingly.

Let's try an example. Imagine that a friend of yours announces that she is about to be married. If you predict that she will be happier and that your friendship will deepen, you may be pleased by the news. If you think her partner is inappropriate for her and suspect that your friendship will suffer, then you may respond negatively. Your reaction will depend on your interpretation of the situation.

Some of the beliefs that you might use to evaluate your friend's news include:

- *"I think that marriage is good for people."*

- *"I think that marriage makes women miserable."*

- *"Our friendship is so weak that any distractions will ruin it."*

- *"He's such a nice guy that she'll obviously prefer to spend all her time with him."*

- *"Everything works out in the end."*

- *"All friendships end in tears."*

- *"I'm unworthy of her friendship."*

We develop our beliefs in a number of ways:

- Some beliefs are taught to us. For example, many parents repeatedly tell their children that they should say "thank you" when someone does something nice for them. Other children are taught less helpful beliefs, like, *"You're the stupid one in the family."*

- We pick up some beliefs by example. For instance, if your mother was afraid of flying, you may have developed the belief that flying is very dangerous. If people around you were aggressive, perhaps you learned that hitting people is a reasonable way of getting things done.

- We pick up some beliefs through our own experiences. For example, if three successive romantic partners had affairs behind your back, you might think all men/women are untrustworthy. If you had an abusive parent, you may have learned that the way to survive is to be as invisible as possible.

Most of the beliefs we have about the world are helpful. Each of us has at least a few distorted ideas, however. Many of these incorrect beliefs were adopted in childhood and are based on the limited perception and powers of reasoning that children have. *"If she said I'm no good, I guess I'm not."* When we find ourselves in situations that activate these ideas (achievement-related situations, for example), we can make grossly distorted appraisals. *"I'll never be any good at this job."* If you find it difficult to be assertive, you may have certain beliefs about assertive behavior that hold you back.

Beliefs that we hold for many years become automatic. You may not even be aware of having them. This does not stop them from influencing your behavior, however. For example, the loss of a parent may have left you with the idea that, *"Everyone I love will abandon me."* Though you may not know you have this belief, it still influences you. You may find it difficult to form close relationships, to trust those to whom you become close, or to relax and enjoy receiving care and attention. A distorted belief can even cause you to bring about the precise consequences you fear. For example, the fear of abandonment may cause you to act in ways that make others give up on you. These experiences can confirm and strengthen your original belief. *"See? I was right."*

How can we deal with unhelpful belief systems? The overriding requirement is that you be aware of your distortions. Until you are aware of a distorted belief, you can do little to change it. Once you know what the belief is, you can take it somewhat less seriously. You may also be able to challenge the belief using your full adult intelligence. *"Wait. I fear abandonment because my mother died when I was seven. That doesn't mean that Joan is going to run off on me. Even if she did, I could handle it better now than I could as a child."* Without awareness, you can do none of this.

Key point: Awareness is the key to dismantling or altering an unhelpful belief system.

Beliefs Related to Assertiveness

Any number of distorted beliefs can cause us to behave in an unassertive manner. Fortunately, many of the most common of these distortions have been identified. The following is a list of some of them. Certain beliefs apply more to people who overuse the passive style. Others apply to those who are too aggressive. Those who use the passive-aggressive style often hold a combination of both types of belief.

As you read the list and the accompanying explanations, consider whether you have each belief. How would you know? An obvious answer is that you might say to yourself, *"What's so distorted about that? That one's true!"* But remember that most of these beliefs are held at an automatic level, and you may not be aware of them. You might think that a certain belief is clearly false, but you hold it anyway.

The real test is whether you behave and react emotionally as though the belief was true. For example, consider this idea: *"I must be perfect, otherwise I am a failure."* You might think that this belief is silly. After all, no one is perfect. But do you go to unreasonable lengths to avoid making little mistakes? Do you feel unusually ashamed when you do make mistakes? Do you avoid trying new activities out of a fear that you won't be able to do them well at first? If so, then you might well be using perfectionistic standards at an automatic level. Even though your adult mind knows that you cannot be perfect and that mistakes are normal, you may have learned as a child that errors were not acceptable. The need to be perfect may prevent you from trying out new assertiveness skills, because you will probably make some mistakes at first. The need to be perfect may also hold you back from revealing your ideas, opinions, and hopes—in case others perceive them as wrong or silly.

As you go through the list below, place a checkmark beside the beliefs that you think you may have. It is important for you to recognize when these beliefs operate so that you can begin to challenge them as they come up.

Beliefs that Support a Passive Role

☐ **Assertiveness means getting your own way all the time.**
Many people believe that assertiveness is all about winning. This holds them back, because they want their relationships to be equal. They don't want to be the boss who decides everything and makes everyone else resentful. This belief confuses assertiveness with aggression. In fact, assertiveness is *not* designed as a surefire strategy for getting your own way. Instead, it is meant to put you on an equal footing with other people. You will not force anyone else to take on your views or preferences or to do your bidding. But, likewise, you will not be forced to do *their* bidding. You will be free to choose what to do, and, often, that choice will be to compromise or give in. But it will be *your* choice what you do, not theirs.

☐ **Being assertive means being selfish.**
Many people have been raised to feel that when they allow their preferences to be known, they are being selfish. These individuals often think it's fine for others to express their preferences, however. Only they themselves have to live up to this rule. The assertive style involves being willing to state your preferences, needs, and opinions, but it does *not* mean demanding that others agree. As well, assertiveness skills are often used on behalf of others ("*I would like Mr. Smith's pain control to be checked every hour, please*") or to find out what others would like ("*Sally, I'd like it if you would to pick the restaurant for tomorrow*").

☐ **Passivity is the way to be loved.**
All human beings crave love and affection. Many of us think that the only way we will be cared for is by adopting a subservient role or by reflecting others' preferences back to them ("*You liked the play? Oh, yes, me too . . . .*"). Is there a way to be yourself and still be loved? Think of the people you care for the most. It probably isn't because they give in to your every whim or because they can't stand up for themselves. Indeed, their self-respect and sense of direction may be precisely what attracts you. Where might someone get the idea that passivity is the way to be loved? Often from past relationships when affection depended on *obedience* (being a good child, doing what you're told) more than personality.

☐ **I am only worthwhile as long as I am doing something for someone else.**

The key word here is *"only."* It is appropriate for us to spend some of our time doing things for other people, and it is fine to receive some of our feelings of self-worth by doing so. But if we take this to the extreme, problems may arise. Do you feel guilty, selfish, or worthless whenever you do something *you* enjoy? Do you feel that it is your role in life to give in to others' requests *every* time? It may be important for you to learn to respect and care for yourself as much as you respect and care for other people. That may mean being more assertive. Otherwise, you may never have the energy to care for other people properly. If the cook doesn't eat, everyone starves.

☐ **The way to be accepted and appreciated by others is to give and give.**

Giving our time and energy for others is appropriate, generous, and positive. But are you trying to buy their affection this way? Many people secretly use a silent contract: *"If I do this for them, they will pay me back."* Unfortunately, the other person is never informed of the bargain or the strings that come with your favors. As a result, they may not do what you had imagined (treat you with respect, go to the movies with you, give you the raise, agree to have sex). Instead, they may just get an uneasy and uncomfortable feeling about the relationship and try to pull back. Excessive and unwanted giving may actually drive people away rather than bringing them closer.

☐ **It's impolite to disagree.**

This is a social rule that many people have adopted. When someone expresses an opinion, no one else is supposed to offer a different one. Whoever comes out with their view first gets to set the tone for everyone. This leads to a lot of awkward conversations in which people who feel differently just smile and nod a lot. It brings discussion to a halt and may lead the person who spoke first to think that everyone else feels the same way. This creates dull conversation. It's usually more interesting if people are willing to contribute their own ideas and views in a relaxed way that does not impose them on everyone else. The fear holding many people back is that expressing your opinion means you have to convince everyone else. You don't.

☐ **If others disagree with me, then I must be wrong.**

Many people grow up feeling that their own ideas and opinions don't matter or that those of others are always better. Do you usually wait for others to express their view before you express yours? If they have views different from yours, do you feel embarrassed or change your opinion? Do you feel that you have no *right* to have an opinion? Having a healthy respect for your own attitudes will allow you to think about and weigh what others say rather than automatically assuming they are correct. It may also enable you to speak up now and then to reveal your own point of view.

☐ **I have to do everything I am asked to do.**

If you believe this, you have to rely on other people not to ask you to do anything unreasonable. You won't feel you have the right to defend yourself or to say "no." Because of this, control over your life is always in the hands of others. People with this belief feel angry and resentful when others make unreasonable requests, but they go along with those requests anyway. They often feel "used" by others. Although it can sometimes be difficult to set and keep boundaries, you have the right to decide for yourself what you will and will not do. You are in charge of your own actions. You have the right to refuse.

☐ **Other people can't handle my assertiveness.**
This belief usually comes from mixing up assertive and aggressive behavior, and results in people taking on a passive style. If you were to give your opinion, or make an objection, or state a preference, then other people would be prevented from saying anything different and their feelings would be hurt. These consequences *are* possible. After all, you don't have control over how others will react. You can, however, make a bad reaction less likely to occur. Ensure that you use an assertive style rather than an aggressive one. Keep relaxed. Make it clear that you are expressing your view, not revealing the only reasonable position. Watch out for the temptation to try to force your view on others. Remind yourself that your goal is to state your view, not to force others to agree.

☐ **If I start speaking up I'll never stop.**
Many people who have a passive style can feel a pressure building up inside of themselves. They are filled with resentment and anger at having their lives controlled by others. They fear what will happen if they begin expressing themselves. Once the monster is loose, will they ever be able to put it back in the box again? There *is* some cause for concern. When some people start opening up they become more aggressive than assertive. It can take a while to develop the skill necessary to be assertive in a positive way. Once we have the skill, however, the pressure no longer builds up to the same extent. We become able to hold back in some situations (perhaps not telling your aunt that you hate her new hairstyle) and move forward in others (giving clear instructions to your own hair stylist).

☐ **It's important to be nice.**
The effect of this belief depends on your definition of the word "nice." If "nice" means giving in to any demand, adopting the views and opinions of others, and avoiding every conflict, then you may have a problem. Assertive behavior can be nice: It is not aggressive and does not trample the rights of others. It also means that you will be the one who decides your own actions.

☐ **My opinion doesn't matter.**
Many people who adopt a passive position do so because they feel that others' views are more important than their own. In certain circumstances, this may be true. A ship captain probably knows more about navigation than you do. A physicist probably knows more about the theory of relativity. However, when it comes to *your* life, *your* actions,

and *your* family, your views are extremely important. They *do* matter. It may be that people around you pay little attention to your opinion—perhaps, in part, because you use a passive style. This may change if you use a different style. Regardless, your views *are* important.

Beliefs Supporting an Aggressive Role

☐ **I'm entitled to be angry.**
Of course you are entitled to be angry. You are entitled to any emotion you feel. You also have the right to express it and rant and rave all you like. The question is this: Will it bring you closer to your goals or take you further away from them? Many people who say they are entitled to be angry really mean, *"I'm entitled to get what I want by expressing my anger"* or *"I'm entitled to explode with anger and have everyone else be completely supportive."* But these beliefs aren't true at all. Expressing anger aggressively will seldom accomplish what we want. Instead, it usually takes us further away from our goals. That may be unjust, but that's the way it is. There's no need to feel guilty for being angry. Anger is a normal emotion. But if you really want what you think you want, you may have to find another way of accomplishing it

☐ **If I'm not aggressive nothing will happen.**
"Nice guys finish last." A lot of people who use the aggressive style hold this belief. In fact, pushing hard and intimidating people often *will* get things done in the short run. Ultimately, however, it makes others resentful and undermines any wish they may have to go along with you. In an employment situation people may quit, become passive-aggressive in return, or sabotage projects. Your reputation will decline. In families, intimidation may help ensure certain chores are completed, but the relationships will suffer and the chores will never be done cheerfully. Assertiveness is quieter, calmer, and more effective in the long run.

☐ **Honesty is the best policy.**
Actually, honesty *is* a pretty good policy. Unfortunately, many people use the idea of honesty as an excuse for being aggressive. *"That opinion is the stupidest thing I've ever heard. And, by the way, are you ever getting fat! Don't get mad, I'm just being honest."* Sometimes, people who use this belief actually fool themselves that they really are "just being honest" and that others are unreasonable for taking offense. In reality, of course, others can see the truth. The hurtful things weren't said out of a desire to be honest. They were meant to hurt. That's why they were said. Honesty is a good policy, but it's not meant to be used as a weapon.

Beliefs Supporting Passive, Aggressive, and Passive-Aggressive Roles

☐ **People should be more considerate.**
Some people believe that they shouldn't *have* to ask, that they shouldn't

need to be assertive. People should know what you feel and what you want and they should take that into account. Well, maybe they should. But they don't. This is a helpless position. You become dependent on others over whom you have no control. When you hold this view you are wishing for another world: a world in which people read your mind and go along with your wishes without questioning you. Unfortunately, none of us live in a world such as that. No one can read our minds, and few people will ever try. Anyway, isn't it a bit inconsiderate to make them *guess* what we want when we could just speak up and *tell* them?

☐ **I'm afraid of trying to be assertive and failing.**
This is a good fear. You *will* fail. Guaranteed. *Everyone* who tries to learn better assertiveness skills has exchanges that don't work out as well as planned. Does this mean that you'll never improve? Of course not. Remind yourself that assertiveness is not all-or-nothing (either you get it or you don't). Assertiveness is a set of skills that takes time and patience to learn. Some people need more time, while others need less. No one *becomes* assertive. They just learn to use the skills more effectively. No matter how little you presently use the assertive style, you can learn to use it more often. Expect a few valuable failures (sometimes called "learning experiences") along the way. If you never fail, well, maybe you're not trying hard enough.

The previous few pages provide only a partial list of common beliefs that hold people back from adopting an assertive style. Can you think of any other beliefs that might be holding you back? Take a moment and write them down.

_____

_____

_____

_____

Checkpoint: The Most Important Belief

Review the last several pages. Pay special attention to the beliefs that you placed a checkmark beside. Which one has the biggest effect on you? Which one holds you back from being assertive the most? Write down this belief in your own words.

_____

_____

Does this belief cause you to become more passive, aggressive, or passive-aggressive?

_____

This belief probably doesn't affect you the same way in all areas of your life. Perhaps it has a bigger effect in romantic relationships, with friends, at work, with your family of origin, or with children. Which relationships does it affect the most? What types of situations are affected?

_____

_____

_____

_____

It is helpful to know what beliefs you are using. In addition, however, you need to *challenge* the belief when it is influencing you. For example, you might counter fears of being assertive by saying to yourself, *"Being unassertive has done more damage to my relationships than being assertive ever could."* You might counter the idea that aggression gets things done by saying, *"Aggression has also driven a lot of people away; assertiveness will let me get things done with less resentment."*

When the belief above begins to affect you, what could you say to yourself in response? Work hard to articulate this belief—it's important.

_____

_____

_____

It is not enough to understand that you are entitled to have your opinions or that you have a right to express them. If you want to weaken the grip that restrictive beliefs have on you, you will have to repeat the revised belief (the one you have written above) over and over to yourself, especially in the situations in which the restrictive belief operates.

Now that you've done the paperwork, assign yourself some homework. Try to catch the belief every time it comes up. Then repeat the more rational alternative to yourself. Don't worry if it sounds false for a while. It probably will. Gradually, the new belief will become part of you.

CHAPTER 5

REALITY CHECK

Many of the barriers that prevent us from being more assertive are in our own heads. We willingly obey imaginary rules that dictate what we are and are not allowed to do. It feels tremendously liberating to realize that the arbitrary standards we set for ourselves are not carved in stone. They do not appear in the criminal code.

The last chapter reviewed many of the maladaptive beliefs that hold us back. Learning to challenge these beliefs when they arise can help us break the grip they have on us. But are there any corresponding beliefs that support assertiveness? Any ideas that can propel us forward?

Yes. But these alternative ideas are not beliefs in the same way that the negative ones are. Negative beliefs represent a distorted view of the world. The corresponding supportive beliefs are designed to overcome distortions, not to impose new ones of their own. They simply recognize the facts. In fact, all of the supportive beliefs boil down to a single basic concept:

Key Point: You are in charge of your behavior; others are in charge of their behavior.

You may feel tempted to argue this point. After all, doesn't the law impose restrictions on us? Don't we have to obey the rules of our jobs, our cultures, or our families? Well, think about it. Every scrap of behavior depends on a brain making certain muscles work: maybe the muscles of your legs, maybe your hands, maybe your mouth. *Whose brain is it?* The brain of the person producing the behavior. Whatever you do, it is you doing it. You are ultimately in charge. Even by most standards of law, your right to control your own behavior applies until your behavior prevents others from having *their* legitimate rights. That leaves you a lot of room.

This idea of personal responsibility doesn't describe anything new. You *already* decide what you will do all the time. For example, perhaps your sister wanted you to organize your parents' wedding anniversary party last year, and you went along with her. You might not be aware of deciding to give in to your sister's demands—but you did. It was, after all, your decision. You could have decided not to give in. The key point above simply says that the decision is yours, whether you know it or not. People act, and their actions are under their own control. This is the reality. *"He told me to and so I had to do it"* is not a statement of fact.

Although you have the right to decide how you will act, others are not obliged to accept, like, or support your decisions. For example, you have the right to change your mind about going to a concert with a friend. Your friend is not required to like it and does not have to respond graciously. Everyone else has the right to decide how they will react to your behavior. Being assertive means making your own decisions about what you will and will not do and accepting the consequences and the responsibility for your behavior.

Accepting the consequences means recognizing that others have the right to react any way they like. If they are critical, your assertive response wouldn't be, *"You shouldn't feel that way"* or *"You can't say that!"* They can feel or say anything they please. You won't try to force them to react in a way that is convenient for you.

Accepting the responsibility means admitting that your actions are your choice. You hold yourself back from saying, *"I had to do it"* or *"They told me to do it"* or *"I had no choice."* You did have a choice, and you made your choice. And you admit it. You don't pretend that it was someone else who broke the vase, or handed in the negative evaluation, or forgot to fill out the requisition form. Acting and then denying responsibility is a passive-aggressive choice, not an assertive one.

A hidden and often poorly understood aspect of assertive behavior is the idea of relinquishing control over others. Just as your actions are under your control (your brain causes them), so too the actions of others are under their control. It is tempting to try to seize control over their behavior, especially when it has an impact on us. But ultimately, our efforts will fail. The frustration of trying and failing to control other people is one of the main causes of anger and aggression.

When this book was in the planning stages, a well-meaning colleague suggested that the subtitle should be, "How to get what you want." This illustrates a classic misconception about assertiveness: the idea that it is all about controlling others and getting them to do (or give you) what you want. Not true. A book with this subtitle would more properly be called *The Aggressiveness Workbook*.

Does this mean that we have to collapse into helplessness when it comes to the behavior of others? Well, yes. And no. And no.

- Yes. We should recognize that ultimately we don't have control over others, that their behavior is under their own control. Knowing this is helpful because it can save us a lot of wasted effort and frustration. We won't take it on ourselves to *try* to control them, because we know we can't.

- No. Recognizing that we don't control others is not really a helpless position. This knowledge prevents us from attempting ultimately futile tasks: controlling how others think, feel, or act. A feeling of helplessness does not come from tasks that we cannot accomplish; it comes from impossible tasks we want to do, try to do, and feel we should be able to do. You seldom feel frustrated that you can't fly like a bird, because you don't feel that you should be able to do so. It is the *belief* that things should be otherwise that causes the frustration.

- And no. Relinquishing control over others does not mean that we give up on having any influence in the world. We can still influence the behavior of others by giving feedback, making requests, and working with our own behavior. In fact, in the long run, we are likely to be *more* effective at influencing others by being assertive than by trying to control them through intimidation. Instead of getting into a spluttering rage with our children, we may simply let them know that we will withhold toy privileges until the chores are done. The choice is theirs. Rather than saying our coworker shouldn't be handing us her own work (controlling her behavior), we can simply inform her that we won't be doing it (controlling our own).

Assertive Responses: A Reality Checklist

On the following pages you will find a list of alternatives to the distorted beliefs of the previous chapter. You can think of these as reality checks. Every one of them is simply a repetition of the key statement at the beginning of this chapter. They repeat over and over again that your behavior is your decision, and others' behavior is up to them.

Some of these ideas are already second nature for you. Others probably give you more trouble. Place a checkmark beside the statements that you particularly need to remember.

☐ **I decide for myself what I will and will not do.**
   Not only are you entitled to decide on your behavior, you already *do* make these decisions. There is a *choice point* between different options (mow the lawn or sit on the deck). This statement simply reminds you to become aware of the choice point. Becoming more assertive does not mean that you refuse to go along with anyone else's wishes. It simply means that when you do so, you recognize that it is a deliberate and conscious choice on your part. *"Joan wants me to help with her shopping when she comes home from the hospital. Though it doesn't sound like much fun, I'll do it because I have the time and I value her friendship."* This is a stronger, more accurate, and more self-respecting position than, *"She asked, so I have to do it."* Because you remember that helping with the shopping was *your* choice, not someone else's, you are less likely to feel resentful and burdened by the task.

☐ **I am my own judge.**
Other people do pass judgment on our thoughts, emotions, actions, and motives. We might as well acknowledge the fact. No law, however, says that you have to agree or go along with their judgment. You are entitled to be your own judge. You may choose to take input from others, if you wish. *"Do you think I should submit my poem to the journal?"* Sometimes, you will judge your own behavior negatively. *"I think Frank was right—I shouldn't have turned down that offer on the house."* The ultimate judgment about your behavior is always yours to make.

☐ **I do not have to justify myself to others.**
When other people want to gain control over you, they will commonly ask you to justify your behavior. *"Tell me why you did it that way."* The idea is that if you cannot come up with a strong enough justification, then you have to go along with their wishes. This puts you in a helpless position and elevates them to the position of control. That is, you appoint them as your judge and plead your case. But *you* are the judge of your actions, not them. You can choose not to offer any reasons, excuses, or justifications. Try to keep this fact in mind the next time you find yourself offering excuse after excuse after excuse. Then hold back on the justifications. Note that this does not mean that you should never provide justifications. You can choose when to justify yourself and when not to. You don't need to keep going until they are convinced. *"Not good enough? Let's see if I can come up with another excuse. . . ."*

☐ **Others do not have to justify themselves to me.**
Sometimes there's nothing wrong with asking for clarification about the reasons for someone's behavior. It's worthwhile, however, to remember that generally others do not have to justify their actions to us. They are entitled to make their own decisions and to use any logic they want. We can get hooked into helpless positions by trying to force others to explain themselves (an aggressive strategy). *"So if you know you shouldn't drink, tell me why you do."* Although it can be very frustrating when others evade our attempts to make them explain themselves, their behavior usually is perfectly legitimate.

☐ **People can ask me anything they want.**
It's true. Look it up. There are no laws against anyone asking you anything at all. *"How much do you make?" "Why'd you choose him for a husband?" "Where did you get that awful haircut?" "Can you help me drain the septic tank Christmas Day?"* We can waste a lot of energy trying to stop people from asking, wishing they wouldn't ask, or feeling enraged that they asked. But they can still ask. Life is much easier if we can mentally give others permission to ask us anything they want. We need not answer, we need not justify ourselves, we need not say yes, and we need not clean any septic tanks. But they can still ask. A question is not a threat.

☐ **My life is my own, and I can turn down requests made by others if I wish.**
Your time and your life are your own. Others can ask you to do

anything and you can say no. Many people feel guilty when they turn down requests. The guilt is a signal that you don't really believe you are entitled to control your own life. Remind yourself that you can indeed say no. The fear may be that you won't live up to the standards of others if you decline their requests. Your behavior, however, will *never* live up to the standards of everyone around you. You are entitled to decide which requests you go along with and which you won't. *"Okay, I will donate to the Heart Fund, but I won't go to the charity ball with Lily."*

☐ **People change their minds.**
Any arguments here? Some people feel that once they make a decision, control over their life passes to someone else. *"Now that I said I'd go sky-diving I don't have any choice; I have to do it."* But when do you *really* have control: before you make a decision or after? Answer: both. When you make a decision about something you don't lose control over your life. Saying you want to go to the lake for the weekend does not mean that the police will take you there in handcuffs if necessary. You still have the right to change your mind. Other people are entitled to be irritated if this happens a lot, but the decision really is yours—even after you've made the initial choice.

☐ **Everyone makes mistakes; this doesn't give control of their lives to others.**
Have you been waiting for the day when you stop making mistakes? Well, give up. That day will never come. You will make mistakes for the rest of your life. Many people feel that if they make mistakes, then others have the right to seize control. *"Your judgment is bad; I'll decide where you should live."* When it's your life, they don't have the right to take control no matter how many mistakes you make. Your brother and your driving instructor have the right to ask you to be more careful, but the act of making a mistake does not put *your* life in *their* hands. Likewise, when others make mistakes, this does not give you control over them. They remain independent human beings—free even to make the same mistake again.

☐ **I don't have to be logical, nor do others.**
No one else is forced to go along with your decisions. Their behavior is under their control. Likewise, you do not have to live up to other people's standards of logic in making decisions about your own life. Some people will try to gain control over you by asking you to explain your logic to them. This is fine. But do you feel that you must either gain the approval of others or change your mind? When it's your life, you have the right to be as illogical as you want. *"Why vacation in Ohio? I just spun the globe and that's where my finger landed."* Other people have the same right. They are under no obligation to explain their behavior to your satisfaction.

☐ **I have the right to be alone.**
Some people assume that if you are not with other people then you are "available" to whomever asks. If you don't have anything specific

planned this evening, you may feel that you have to agree to their invitations. But you don't. Everyone needs some solitary or unstructured time—including you. You can decide for yourself whether you want to be with other people—even if they really want your company. Similarly, they need time off too. Keeping this principle in mind can help us avoid feeling hurt or frustrated when others turn down our invitations in favor of time alone.

☐ I don't know everything, and I don't have to.

Who appointed you to be the encyclopedia? You don't know everything, you never will, and no one can force you to try. When you don't understand something, do you feel you have to hide the fact? Are you unable to ask for clarification? In most circumstances it's okay not to know or understand something. It's usually fine to ask. In fact, inquiry usually leads to a better outcome than if you pretend to understand when you don't. Of course, your boss still has the right to be annoyed if you don't know where the Smith file is.

☐ I have my opinions and convictions, and others have theirs.

To hold a certain attitude or belief, you don't have to convince the people around you to hold the same view. You have the right to your convictions even if others do not share them. This doesn't necessarily mean that your view is correct, but you do have the right to your own ideas. Similarly, others have a right to hold their views even if they cannot explain them to your satisfaction.

☐ I have the right to protest unfair treatment or criticism.

No law states that you have to keep your mouth shut if you are treated unfairly. Sometimes speaking up may not help as much as you would like. You may be surprised, however, how open some people are when you speak up assertively (rather than aggressively). It is almost always difficult to stand up for yourself when you are being treated poorly. Keep in mind, though, that things seldom get better when you give your silent approval and passively go along with bad situations.

☐ I have the right to ask for help or emotional support.

In difficult times, most of us need help of some kind. Interestingly, many of us are very reluctant to ask for it. Most often this comes from a fear of being a burden on others. Sometimes this is justified—even though the people we ask always have the right to say "no." Just as often, asking for help can bring relationships closer. Consider how you might feel if you received a specific, time-limited request for help from a friend. You might welcome it as a way to get to know the person better and develop a deeper friendship.

☐ Others can give advice, but they don't make my decisions.

When you ask someone's advice about something, does this mean that they make your decision for you? No. Typically you are asking for information that you can use in making your decision. You are not handing the decision to them. They might provide information that convinces you to make the choice they would make. Or, perhaps, another option will remain more attractive to you. The final decision is still yours. Of course, this counts double when people give you advice that you did not ask for. Similarly, others have every right to ask you for advice, hear it, and make the opposite decision from what you've suggested. If you like, you can take this as a sign of how little they think of you, how worthless you are, and how inconsiderate they are, and you can become very angry. That's up to you, though it's typically a waste of your effort. They didn't ask you to make the decision, they asked you for information.

☐ I am not responsible for other people's problems.

When someone tells you about a problem they are having, do you experience a sense of pressure to solve it for them? Are there people in your life who try to hand their problems to you? *"Mom, I left my bike at school and now I only have five minutes to get to my practice."* Generally speaking, you are under no obligation to take over other people's problems for them, nor do you have to come up with a workable solution. There are some limits here, of course: If your child has broken her arm, you are obliged to seek help for her. But these exceptions are more rare than many of us think. Taking on other people's problems may not be the best thing for them anyway. Some people need to learn to take responsibility for themselves. *"Well then, you'd best walk back to school to get your bike and ride over to the practice."*

☐ Others are not responsible for solving my problems.

It can be tempting to blame others for our problems and to insist that they take primary responsibility for solving them. They don't have to do so. This is a central issue with the passive-aggressive style and, most often, is a holdover from childhood, when Mom or Dad would take charge if things went wrong. As adults, if we have a problem it is generally up to us to do something about it. Trying to make others take it on places us in a helpless position because we are not in control of their behavior. If finding a solution is really that important, it's best that we get to it, rather than waiting for others to do so.

☐ Direct is usually better.

We often feel nervous about asking for help, giving feedback, protesting unfair decisions, and declining requests. We find ourselves in approach-avoidance conflicts: We want to get our way (approach) but we don't want to take responsibility for voicing it (avoidance). The solution we sometimes fall into is passive-aggressive behavior, which allows us to do both. We get to avoid cleaning the garage by "forgetting" to do it rather than accepting responsibility by saying, *"No, I'm not going to do that."* The avoidant strategy often works—in the short run. But passive-aggressive behavior undermines us in the long run. People become resentful, we gain a reputation for being unreliable, and life generally grows worse. The direct, nonaggressive, assertive approach is usually more effective.

Checkpoint: The Reality Check Challenge

Review the list of statements above. You probably found a few that you have a hard time believing, and this holds you back from being more assertive. Which one gives you the most trouble? Write it out in your own words.

_____

_____

Everyone can think of exceptions to some of the principles. You don't really have the right to yell "fire" in a crowded theater, for example. We hope our pilot doesn't believe that forgetting to put down the landing gear is allowed. In your life, there are probably circumstances in which the statement you have identified may be limited. There are probably other times when it applies and you have a hard time acting accordingly. What are the situations that give you trouble regarding this statement?

_____

_____

_____

What do you do instead?

_____

_____

What would you like to do?

_____

_____

_____

What could you tell yourself when you are next in those situations? How could you remind yourself that behaving assertively is an option?

_____

_____

_____

Try to keep this new way of thinking in mind for at least the coming week. When you find yourself in one of the difficult situations you have identified, make sure that you fill out an Assertiveness Scorecard (see the Introduction) to evaluate how you handled it.

CHAPTER 6

ON THE LAUNCHPAD: PREPARING FOR CHANGE

By now you know about the different styles of interpersonal behavior: passive, aggressive, passive-aggressive, and assertive. You have identified the styles you overuse and the areas in which you need to become more assertive. You are familiar with some of the common barriers to assertive behavior. You know that your body's stress response, your gender, and the other people in your life can all act to hold you back from being as assertive as you would like to be. You know that your personal history has likely given you some negative beliefs about assertiveness, about social relationships, and about your place in the world, beliefs that lose some of their power once you become aware of them. And you have considered some alternative ideas that you can use to overcome distortions. Perhaps now you are ready to start trying out some new skills and strategies.

Well, almost.

Before we get to the assertiveness skills, there are a few last steps to consider. You need to lay the groundwork for change in your life. In this chapter you will find a series of ideas that will help to set the stage. Some are suggestions for ways to think about assertiveness, relationships, and change. Some are concrete suggestions for action that apply no matter which of the assertiveness skills you are practicing. All are worthwhile to consider before you really get started.

Assertiveness Is What You Do, Not Who You Are

Some people say, *"I'm just not the assertive type. Never have been, never will be."* This idea assumes that assertiveness is a kind of personal characteristic, like intelligence or height. It further assumes that assertiveness is all-or-nothing. Some people have it, others don't. You may believe that you're one of the people who don't, and nothing you do will change things. This statement doesn't quite reflect reality.

It is true that the assertive style doesn't come naturally to everyone. Some people have an easier time using an assertive style than others do. Perhaps some of the reason for this is inborn. It might be partly due to upbringing. If you grew up in a family in which being assertive was punished, you may have learned to avoid trying to be assertive.

But assertiveness is really a set of skills, not a type of person. And like most skills, they can be learned. Imagine someone saying, *"I can't drive a car, I'm just not the type."* It might be true that they have never learned, that they don't like cars, or that they have no need of a car, but they could probably learn to drive if they wanted to do so. The ability to drive is not a personality trait. Neither is assertiveness.

Some people try being assertive and notice that it feels awkward. Like any other skill, new assertiveness strategies *will* feel awkward for a while. Unnatural. False. It can be tempting to use this as a sign that assertiveness is wrong for you. Don't.

If you can drive, think of how awkward it felt the first time you got behind the wheel of a car. Gradually, it became more familiar. Now it may feel as though the car is actually a part of you, as though you *wear* it as much as you sit in it. Driving has become second nature. Assertiveness skills are similar. Gradually they become more comfortable as you become better at using them. Part of the task of learning assertiveness skills is to tolerate the early period when you feel awkward using them.

Allow Errors

In this process of learning to become more assertive, consciously give yourself permission to make mistakes—because you *will* make them. Allow it to happen. Be willing to take risks. When mistakes happen, remind yourself that you are *supposed* to be making them. Errors are vitally important. They are opportunities to fine-tune your skills.

Why do you need to remind yourself of something so obvious? Because many people who underutilize the assertive style avoid taking risks. Difficult interpersonal situations activate the stress response, which is designed to take us away from risk and toward safety. Unfortunately, stress promotes aggressive and avoidant strategies. Assertiveness involves becoming more comfortable with risk and allowing errors to occur.

So, try to catch yourself saying, *"What if I make a mistake?"* This question falsely assumes that there is some possibility you won't make mistakes. There isn't. You *will* make at least one. A better question is: *"When will I make mistakes (plural) and how can I remind myself to make the most of them?"*

Start Easy

You wouldn't expect to become an expert tennis player in one day. And you wouldn't try competing against a champion the first time you picked up a racquet. Instead, you would allow yourself some time to learn the basics. Only later would you feel ready to participate in a difficult match.

Similarly, assertiveness skills take time to master. It can be tempting, though, to rush out and use them with the most difficult people and situations that you face. Then, just as you might expect if you were to play your first tennis game at Wimbledon, the result is disappointing.

A better strategy is to take your time and practice the basics first. One way to do this is to break assertiveness skills into their components. For example, you might start by practicing an assertive posture or vocal tone, perhaps in front of the mirror. Then you could gradually combine the skills until you feel ready to try them out with someone. This workbook encourages such a strategy by introducing new skills a bit at a time, starting with the skills that people often find easier to learn.

Another aspect of this approach is to start by practicing assertiveness in easier situations and then gradually work your way up to the difficult ones. This means that you must temporarily give up on the most difficult situations.

Perhaps you have some especially challenging situations or relationships in your life right now. These may constitute the main reasons you're working on this book. Name one or two of these pressing situations in the spaces below.

1. _____

_____

2. _____

_____

It is important for you to leave these situations alone until you are more prepared to deal with them. Even though you may really want to confront your boss or your spouse on a big, emotionally charged issue, it is best to wait until you have had a chance to practice being assertive in easier situations.

So, come up with a couple of easier situations to work on. Name two situations that you find much less challenging than the ones you listed above. These should be situations that give you a little difficulty but which, generally, you believe you can handle.

1. _____

_____

2. _____

_____

You may find that you're a bit resistant to focusing your efforts on these situations because they are no big deal. They don't bother you much. Remember that there are two reasons for working on them. First, they still cause you some trouble. Second, they will be good practice before you challenge bigger situations—dealing with the issues you identified first.

Keep these issues in mind as you prepare to practice the skills outlined in the upcoming chapters.

It's Not Necessary to Be Assertive All the Time

If you know how to drive a car, this doesn't mean that you *must* drive wherever you go. It only means that you *can* drive, if you wish. Similarly, knowing how to be assertive doesn't mean that you have to be assertive in every situation. It only means that you *could* be assertive, if you wanted to be.

Some situations require more assertiveness than others. When you are at a kindly elderly relative's home, you might accept a cup of tea even though you don't really want it. When a thief with a gun asks you for money, you might just give it to him. When your hang-gliding instructor orders you to fasten your harness, you might meekly obey. When you are safe and when the issue is important to you, however, assertiveness generally leads to better results than the alternatives. Your goal in learning assertiveness skills should be to have the assertive *option*, even if you do not use it.

Consider Your Timing

Some people think of the right thing to say *after* the discussion is over. They get talked into things and then regret their choices later. Is this you?

In most situations, you have the right to delay your answers. If you realize that you would like to be more assertive but can't think of what to say, ask for time. Use phrases like, *"I can't answer that right now,"* or *"I'll let you know next Tuesday."* This will provide you the time you need to think the situation through. As assertiveness becomes a habit, you will get faster at formulating the responses you want.

For practice, set aside a few days in which you will not agree to *any* requests immediately. Whenever anyone asks you to do something, tell them you will let them know at some later time. For example, you can say:

- *"I'll call you back in a few minutes about that."*

- *"I'll tell you at the end of the meeting."*

- *"Let me check my schedule and get back to you."*

- *"Let me think a moment."*

- *"I'll tell you on Thursday."*

Make sure you *do* respond to them in the agreed upon time, and feel free to go along with the request. The exercise is to insert a delay rather than to say a flat "no." Saying "no" can be much harder and is covered in chapter 13.

Strike While the Iron Is Cool

When you or the person you are speaking with is upset, it can be difficult for either of you to express appropriate, calm, and assertive responses. You will usually find that the discussion goes better when you are both more relaxed. It may be appropriate to postpone your discussion until you have both had a chance to cool down.

If you have limited time to make a decision, you may need to perform a strategy designed to help you regain your focus. Here are some options:

- Perform the diaphragmatic breathing exercise discussed in chapter 2. Only try this if you've been practicing the exercise, however. It takes a while to get good enough at diaphragmatic breathing to calm yourself down in a tense situation.

- Exercise. The stress response is designed to prepare you for vigorous physical activity. So do some. Exercise can help to "burn out" the stress response, leaving you feeling calmer and able to think more clearly about your response to the situation.

- Create some physical distance. Go for a walk, sit in another room (especially one in which you normally feel secure and comfortable), or, if necessary, hide out in a washroom cubicle for a while. Don't stay in there forever, though. You're trying to gain some perspective and think, not become a hermit.

The recommendation to take some time to cool down comes with two caveats. First, sooner is usually better than later. If you put off a discussion until the issue is in the distant past, neither of you may be able to remember what you were talking about. *"Jinold, do you remember asking me to take over the Johnson file last year?"* As well, unexpectedly bringing up an issue that bothered you a month ago can come across as odd or petty to others. *"Marybeth, when you ordered me to drive you to your dog's veterinarian's office last month, I felt that it wasn't in my job description."*

Second, some people may *never* become calm and rational. You probably have some control over how upset *you* become, and a cooling-off period may help. But you have no control over the emotions of others. They may become upset the moment the matter is raised. If the issue is important to you and if your personal safety is assured, you may have to deal with the matter anyway—even if the other person's emotions are running high.

The Bonsai Principle

Good assertive communication is usually more precise than the alternatives. Consider the statement: *"I wish you had called to let me know that you were going to be late."* This assertion communicates exactly what is bothering you. Avoidance of the issue (the passive option) shuts down the communication before it begins. Cold, brooding silence (the passive-aggressive option) leaves the reason for your displeasure a mystery and invites the other person to ignore it altogether or to guess what you mean (and maybe feel resentful that you don't just tell them). Aggressive responses, such as, *"You have no consideration for me!"*, focus on the person's character rather than on what's really bothering you: their lateness.

Being precise can be difficult. It is often tempting to go into a long, long explanation of *exactly* what we mean. One participant in an assertiveness group wrote down exactly what she wanted to say to a coworker about an issue. She came up with a twenty-two–page letter!

Long explanations are usually a bad idea. The other person is unlikely to pay attention to most of it, and they can feel assaulted by the amount of detail you are giving. As well, a long explanation is often a *justification* of our behavior, wants, and expectations. *"I really need you to do this because of . . . and . . . and . . . and. . . ."* Justifications encourage the other person to challenge your reasons rather than deal with your statement or request. As a consequence, we have a general principle of assertive communication:

Key Point: Shorter is better than longer.

Why is this called the *bonsai principle*? Your communication should be like a bonsai: trimmed down to the basics.

One strategy is to write down what you want to say in note form. Like the letter-writing client, when you first do this you will almost always go into too much detail and repeat yourself. Once you have your ideas down on paper, however, you can take your time trimming it down. Eventually, you will have a message that says what you mean without going on and on. Imagine that you are a gardener, gradually clipping away everything that is not essential.

Who's in Charge Here?

Remember: *You are in charge of your own behavior. Others are in charge of their behavior.* In this respect, only the assertive style is based in reality. It enables us to control our own actions while leaving the actions of others up to them.

The passive style is based on the belief that others control us. We fail to see the options available to us and, instead, attempt to pass control over to the other person. We do what the other person wants, then feel that they were responsible for our actions. *"I couldn't help it—it wasn't up to me."* We may also place others in a position of judgment over us by explaining and justifying our own behavior. *"Oh, I went to that bar because it was the closest and because Francois insisted and because. . . ."* All of this is an illusion. Responsibility for our actions remains with us. After all, whose legs did the walking, anyway? Whose voice did the speaking? Whose hands wrote the letter? If they were yours, then you were the one in charge.

The aggressive style is based on the idea that we can control others. When we behave aggressively, we often attempt to seize control of others' behavior. *"You'll do what I tell you to do!"* We also feel entitled to offer firm advice about how others should run their lives. *"Oh no, you don't want that dress, trust me."*

Then we become offended if they don't treat our word as though it were divinely inspired. We may also feel entitled to pass judgment on their past behavior and believe that they should accept our judgment. *"Look at you! You don't even look guilty for not doing what I told you!"* Any sense of control we gain in these situations is an illusion. The other person remains fully in control of and responsible for their own behavior.

The passive-aggressive style combines the worst of both worlds. We avoid taking responsibility for our own behavior (*"The fax machine must have eaten your message . . ."*) while trying to control the behavior of others (*". . . so I guess you'll have to do it yourself"*). This style is completely off base: We believe that we can decide what others do, we avoid taking charge of our own behavior, and we're dishonest about both.

The assertive style gets it right: We accept responsibility for our own behavior, we decide what we will and will not do, and we leave the behavior of others in their own hands.

The assertive style sometimes seems like a good way to take charge of a situation. It is usually better to see it as a way to take charge of *ourselves*. As you work through the skills in this manual, you will read a number of examples in which people try to a) give control away to others, or b) take control from others. We will constantly return to the idea of knowing the boundaries of our control. We are responsible for ourselves; others are responsible for themselves.

Using Humor

Can you use humor when being assertive? Absolutely. In fact, humor is often one of the most useful ways of being assertive without coming across to others as aggressive. There are some guidelines, however:

- Humor is most likely to be misinterpreted by people who do not know you well. It may be best to avoid using much humor when being assertive with strangers.

- If you usually have a passive style, you may feel tempted to use self-deprecating humor. *"I know it's completely irresponsible of me—as is so often the case—but could I possibly take the day off tomorrow?"* Although self-deprecating humor can be both funny and appropriate, when you are trying to be assertive it invites others not to take you seriously. Save this type of humor for other situations.

- Humor doesn't usually work as well when those you are speaking to are angry. They may miss the humorous aspect completely (*"Well, you're right, you are irresponsible!"*) or they may be offended that you're not taking their point seriously (*"This isn't a joke, you know"*).

- Watch for hidden aggression in your own humor. If you are feeling angry, you may insert small attacks in your humor without meaning to do so. *"Ha, ha, I'm as likely to do that as you are to regrow your hair!"*

Pick a Model

When you want to become more assertive, it can be hard to decide how to act and what to say. Any new skill requires time and practice to master, and many of us find it difficult to evaluate our own behavior. It can help to think of someone in your life who is assertive in a way that you admire and ask yourself, *"How would _____ react in this situation?"*

Your goal is not to become "just like them." After all, you are an individual. Sometimes you may decide that you want to do exactly what they would do; sometimes you will want to change it to make the behavior your own. The point is to give yourself an idea of what to do when you feel stuck. It can also help to think of more than one such person so that you acquire a range of ideas from which to choose.

Name two people who have assertive styles that you like.

1. _____

2. _____

Keep these people in mind as you practice new skills. When you find yourself stuck or are trying to come up with a way to respond to a situation, think of what they would do. Then ask yourself whether their imagined response is similar to what you would like to do. If so, adapt it to your style and put it into action. Gradually it will become your own style.

Isn't this cheating? Isn't the whole point of this workbook to find your own style and express your own uniqueness? Well, yes, that is the point, but the strategy isn't cheating. Your goal isn't to adopt the other person's style completely. One of the main ways we learn how to behave, however, is by watching the behavior of others. They serve as models to us and we benefit from their example. We watch the golf pro and try to imitate her swing. We watch the television chef and create a similar dish. We listen to the kayaking instructor's description of the correct stroke and do it for ourselves. None of this forfeits who we are. Learning the skills simply gives us new avenues for expressing ourselves.

Consider Your Safety

Whenever you are thinking about being assertive you should consider your personal safety. Specifically:

- Is it safe for me to be in this situation?

- Is it safe for me to behave assertively while I am in it?

Responding assertively to an armed mugger, for instance, could endanger your life. Taking your blind date home could put you in danger, no matter how assertive you are. Becoming assertive while you are alone with a violent spouse or family member could be extremely unwise. When you behave assertively you are taking back control over your own life. If the person you are with wants to retain that control, they could become violent.

This workbook is not intended to be an instructional manual for people in abusive relationships. It does not provide all of the considerations that you may need to take into account to deal with such a situation. If you are in a violent relationship, it may be extremely important for you to seek extra help or counseling.

Are there situations in your own life in which being assertive (or changing your style) could lead to actual violence? If so, make a brief note of them here.

Make a conscious decision now to set these situations aside and not use them for your practice exercises in the upcoming chapters. Wait until you have developed adequate strategies to keep yourself safe before you put them into action. Even once you are comfortable being assertive, be particularly careful when you're in the situations you've listed above.

Cultural Factors

This guide is written from the perspective of North American culture. Every culture differs in terms of the amount of assertiveness that is considered appropriate and the way that it is expressed. The same behavior can be viewed as assertive in one culture, passive in another, and inexcusably aggressive in a third. As a consequence, some of the recommendations and the wording of the examples may be inappropriate for other cultures. This includes cultures outside North America and some cultures within it (for example, many aboriginal cultures). Styles of nonverbal behavior may be particularly different from culture to culture.

What does *not* differ, however, is that some degree of assertive behavior is appropriate in virtually every culture. In almost every culture there are individuals who behave in an inappropriately aggressive manner and others who are needlessly passive. These individuals can benefit from learning more about the boundaries of appropriate assertiveness in their own group, culture, or country. The concept of assertiveness, then, is universal. If you are from another culture you may have to investigate the degree to which the concepts expressed in this workbook are appropriate.

PART TWO

BECOMING ASSERTIVE

CHAPTER 7

BECOMING VISIBLE:
NONVERBAL BEHAVIOR

Television and movies give us information in two ways: in sound and in pictures. Similarly, when we communicate with other people we usually do so in two ways at the same time.

The *verbal* channel contains the words that make up our intended message. This channel tells our audience what we are talking about. Whether we communicate out loud, in writing, or by sign language, this channel is almost always used. Many assertiveness skills focus on the way to word our messages to produce the best outcome.

The *nonverbal* channel is made up of our posture, our movements, and our voice tone while delivering the verbal message. Although this channel is not too important when we communicate in writing, it is vital when we talk face-to-face or on the phone. In fact, your impact often depends more on *how* you say things than on *what* you say.

Which channel is most important? That depends on which part of the communication you are thinking about. If you are focusing on the actual informational content, then the verbal channel is usually most important. *"How do I set the time on this VCR?"* A person's nonverbal behavior in information-focused situations such as this won't tell you much.

If you want to know about anything other than the straight facts, however, then the nonverbal channel is usually more important: *"Does he look down on me for not knowing how to set the VCR's time?" "Is he angry that I interrupted his studying to ask?" "Does he care whether the time is set properly?" "Does he really know or is he guessing?"* In all of these cases, you are likely to pay more attention to the nonverbal content than to what the person actually says. This is a good idea: Usually the information you gain from paying attention to the nonverbal channel is more complete and accurate than the information from the verbal channel would be. People learn a lot from accurately assessing nonverbal style, including:

- Your emotional state at the time

- How you feel about the issue being discussed

- How you feel toward the person with whom you are speaking

- Whether you believe the issue at hand is important

- Your level of confidence in what you are saying

- Whether you expect your words to have an impact

- Whether you see yourself as equal, inferior, or superior to the other person

Sometimes your words and your nonverbal behavior communicate the same message (for example, confidence and an expectation that an issue can be resolved). At other times your verbal and nonverbal messages may differ. Consider the following examples. Think about what you would believe in each case.

Verbal	Nonverbal
"I love you."	Distant, looking downward and away
"I know you can do it."	Tentative voice, halting speech, forced smile
"I'm not going."	Pulling coat on, walking toward door
"I'm not angry."	Said loudly, teeth gritted, followed by muttered obscenity.
"Great presentation."	Exaggerated emphasis on "great," eyes rolling, skeptical look.
"A lovely gift; I'm pleased."	Quickly setting gift aside, barely glancing at it.
"Thanks a lot."	Listless voice, looking distracted, emphasis on "lot."

When your verbal and nonverbal messages differ, your audience is more likely to believe the nonverbal message. They may also react in a negative way to your entire attempt to communicate.

When you decide to talk about an issue, you always choose your words. Sometimes you may even plan out in advance what you want to say. You may not pay as much attention, however, to your nonverbal behavior. As a result you may sometimes communicate more than you intend. For example, while asking the boss for a raise you may make it clear by your actions that you don't really expect to receive one. At other times, your behavior may communicate something that isn't true. A habit of looking away may communicate anxiety even when you are calm. A habit of holding tension in your jaw may communicate anger that you don't feel. Consequently, it is worthwhile to practice nonverbal communication so that you can express what you really mean.

Assertive Nonverbal Communication

An assertive nonverbal style communicates respect for yourself and the other person. It signals an expectation that your point of view will be heard. A passive style places the other person in charge and communicates an expectation that your views will go unheard. An aggressive style communicates a lack of respect for the other person and what they have to contribute. The passive-aggressive style usually looks passive but hides a secret aggressive motivation.

Before exploring the different styles further, let's consider a few concepts that will be useful:

- **Face plane**: An imaginary flat surface defined by your chin and your eyes. If you like, you can imagine a card or a piece of paper stuck on the end of your nose. The card is vertical when you look directly at someone, tilted back when you raise your chin, and tilted forward when you drop your chin to your chest.

- **Body plane**: An imaginary flat surface defined by the front of your shoulders and hips. When you stand or sit up straight your body plane is vertical. When you slouch back the body plane is angled upward. When you sit forward, elbows on knees, your body plane is tilted downward.

- **Personal space**: An imaginary bubble of space surrounding a person. The boundaries are defined by the discomfort an individual feels when someone else (other than an intimate friend or partner) enters the space. In Western cultures, the personal space typically extends forward from one to two and a half feet and is somewhat less at the back and sides. The normal amount of personal space varies from culture to culture. Generally, personal space is larger in more northern cultures (e.g., Great Britain) and is smaller in cultures located closer to the equator (e.g., Brazil). Cultural variations in personal space can produce discomfort and awkwardness when members of different cultures communicate.

Checkpoint: Nonverbal Styles

The following pages provide a list of the main aspects of nonverbal behavior. Descriptions are given for the assertive, passive, and aggressive styles. (Again, the passive-aggressive style most often uses a passive nonverbal style.) For each aspect, identify how you most commonly behave when you are in a situation involving mild conflict (such as returning an undercooked meal at a restaurant, saying "no" to a request for your time, or requesting an extension on a deadline). Place a checkmark beside the description that fits your style the best. Don't be too surprised if your answers are similar for many of the items. These different aspects of our nonverbal communication tend to go together.

Posture

☐ **Assertive:** An upright posture with the shoulders back. The body plane is vertical and generally faces the other person directly. The face plane is also vertical (tilted neither up nor down) and is aimed more or less directly at the other person.

☐ **Passive:** The body is hunched, as though you want to make yourself smaller than you really are. The body plane is usually pointed to one side of the other person and may lean away or toward the ground. The face plane is often angled downward and away. Shoulders may be raised toward the ears. Your head may be lowered like a turtle's. The body seems either tense or defeated.

☐ **Aggressive:** The posture may be large and threatening, or crouched as though you are a tiger ready to pounce. The body plane is often angled downward and toward the other person. The face may be angled toward the other person or tilted upward toward the ceiling (the nose in the air). Overall, this posture communicates that you are ready for a fight.

Movements and Gestures

☐ **Assertive**: Movements are usually relaxed and fluid. There is little muscle tension. Gestures are natural, open, and relaxed. The hands are usually relaxed and open rather than grasping one another or balled up in fists.

☐ **Passive:** This varies from person to person. Some people gesture little when they are being passive. They look depressed and lethargic. Others speed up when they adopt the passive style, making quick but unfocused gestures (fluttering hands, fidgeting, playing with coins or buttons). Some people make classic "don't attack me" movements, shrugging the shoulders and making helpless gestures with the hands, palms outward. Showing the palms is a classic passive gesture.

☐ **Aggressive:** The body tension associated with this style is revealed by physical gestures, which tend to be rapid and sharp. The person may gesture with the index finger pointed. Alternatively, all the fingers may be extended stiffly together. Sometimes the hand is used in short striking or karate-chopping motions. The closer these motions are to the other individual's personal space, the more aggressive the gesture.

Physical Distance

☐ **Assertive:** Interpersonal distance differs a great deal from culture to culture. People using the assertive style during conflict usually maintain their normal conversational distance (i.e., the same distance they use in situations not requiring assertive behavior).

☐ **Passive:** The interpersonal distance is usually greater than normal (unless the quiet voice makes standing close essential). Combined with the turned-away body posture, this distance makes passive individuals look as though they want to escape from the interaction.

☐ **Aggressive:** The interpersonal distance is often closer than usual, invading the other person's space. The broad and rapid gestures that are often used may cause the hands or face to suddenly lunge toward the other person.

Eye Contact

☐ **Assertive:** Eye contact is frequent but is broken by occasional horizontal glances away.

☐ **Passive:** Eye contact is usually avoided. The eyes tend to be cast downward. When eye contact is made, it's usually done by looking up rather than by lifting the head.

☐ **Aggressive:** Eye contact is usually direct and fixed. Considerable muscle tension is usually held around the eyes, resulting in a squinting or glaring look. A person unused to being aggressive may have the same tension around the eyes but look away from the other person.

Facial Expression

☐ **Assertive:** The facial expression is appropriate to the content of the message. If the discussion is serious or confrontational, the person will typically smile less often than usual. Regardless, the face generally communicates openness via a direct gaze, a calm expression, and little muscle tension. The teeth are slightly apart and the forehead is usually smooth.

☐ **Passive:** The expression is often anxious or apologetic. Considerable tension is likely to be evident, particularly in the forehead. The person may flush. Nervous smiling or inappropriate laughter is common for some people.

☐ **Aggressive:** The face generally holds significant muscle tension, often most noticeably in the jaw. The expression tends to be fixed rather than rapidly changing, is often recognizably angry, and glaring (directed toward the other person or away) is common. Reddening is likely but is usually distinguishable from a blush (sometimes by being somewhat blotchier) unless the person is unused to being aggressive, in which case blushing may occur.

Physical Contact

☐ **Assertive:** Physical contact varies tremendously from culture to culture. During an assertive exchange, the individual will generally touch the other person no more nor less than is usual for them in other situations. When touching occurs, it is usually gentle and intended to express empathy for the other person. In cultures that do not often touch, gentle open-handed patting gestures against the edge of the other person's personal space (or against a table or the arm of a chair in the direction of the person) may be common.

☐ **Passive:** Touching is usually minimal because passive people retreat into themselves. If used at all, physical touch tends to communicate *"Don't hate me"* or *"Don't hurt me."*

☐ **Aggressive:** Touching, if present, may be firm and jabbing (as with an accusing finger). Some people, of course, become physically violent. More often, the aggressive person will make rapid gestures (including pointing and hand jabbing) close to the other person, but without touching them. It may look as though the person is attempting to pierce the bubble of the other's interpersonal space.

Voice Tone

☐ **Assertive:** The voice is warm and well modulated. It may be firm if the situation requires gravity, but the message is seldom delivered through gritted teeth. The volume is normal.

☐ **Passive:** The voice is often quiet, sometimes to the point that others cannot hear. The tone may be complaining, particularly during self-justifications or attempts to pacify the other person. Statements may have an upswing at the end, as though the person is asking a question. *"So, I'd like a raise?"* This "question-talking" represents a significant difficulty for many individuals. It communicates uncertainty and openness to being influenced.

☐ **Aggressive:** Some individuals exhibit a "hot voice" by yelling and shouting, with lots of emotion and volume. *"How could you do this! I can't believe it!"* Others typically have a colder style, the words being squeezed out between gritted teeth with little emotional variation. *"I. Want. It. Done. Now. Understand?"* The volume of a colder voice may be hostile and loud or icy and threateningly quiet and often has a sarcastic or condescending tone.

Fluency

☐ **Assertive:** The flow of words is even and conversational, without rushing or hesitating. That said, anyone can speak assertively, no matter what their usual conversational style might be. The main point is that the person's usual fluency doesn't typically change much during an assertive encounter. The low stress level associated with the assertive style doesn't interfere with the production of fluent speech.

☐ **Passive:** There may be considerable hesitation caused partly by stress and partly by a search for the words that will satisfy the other person. Sentences are often left incomplete. *". . . and I wanted to ask you if . . . because I'm so busy that . . . and Aunt Florence arrives Friday. . . ."* There may also be much pausing and stalling before getting to the point: *". . . so I thought, well, you know . . . I mean. . . ."* The pace is often slow, or speech may pour out in an anxious rush.

☐ **Aggressive:** The pace of speech may be slower than usual (through gritted teeth and with a cold expression) or faster (usually with increased volume and sharp gestures). Some people become less fluent when angry (the "spluttering rage"). More commonly, though, there is little hesitation. Fluency may be less of a problem than with the passive style because the aggressive person is less worried about offending others.

Physical Appearance

☐ **Assertive:** Clothing, hairstyle, glasses, tidiness, and so on are all expressions of ourselves. The assertive person is able to adapt to the situation (for example, by dressing up if the occasion demands it), but this is not designed either to seek anonymity (by wearing what everyone else wears) or to intimidate others. Assertive people may be conscious of the impact their appearance has on people (perhaps taking some time to find a hairstyle that looks good), but the look is chosen at least in part to reflect the person's own preferences and personality.

☐ **Passive:** The most common passive style is designed to help the person blend with a group. Clothing, glasses, and hairstyle are all carefully chosen to avoid standing out, the product of a fear of what might happen if the person was more visible, distinctive, or honest. Some people use glasses, makeup, or beards as barriers to hide behind (though others find them to be comfortable expressions of their personalities).

☐ **Aggressive:** Clothes, hairstyle, and accessories (including glasses, watch, and even car) may be chosen deliberately to intimidate others or to communicate power. Others aggressively rebel against expectations, choosing styles mainly for their ability to provoke people (for example, wearing jeans to a formal wedding out of a desire to displease rather than as an honest expression). Extreme or unusual styles are not aggressive or passive-aggressive in themselves—the key is the *reason* the styles are chosen.

Checkpoint: The Self-Assessment

Now go back over each of the categories of nonverbal behavior. Total the number of checkmarks you placed beside each communication style, and enter them below:

_____ Assertive

_____ Passive

_____ Aggressive

This isn't a formal test to determine which style you use most often. If the majority of your checkmarks fall in the passive or aggressive categories, however, then perhaps your nonverbal communication style needs some attention.

Review the categories again. Which of the categories of nonverbal behavior (e.g., posture, vocal tone, appearance) causes you the most trouble when you are trying to be assertive?

_____

Which style do you tend to use instead: passive or aggressive?

_____

As you practice assertive nonverbal behavior, it may be important for you to pay particular attention to this one aspect of your style.

On the pages that follow, you will find exercises designed to help you to adopt a more assertive nonverbal style.

Practice Session: A Week of Action

In this exercise you will work on *one* of the categories of nonverbal behavior that causes you trouble. The goal will not be for you to become completely assertive in all areas of your life. Instead, you will allow most of your nonverbal behavior to stay pretty much the way it already is. You need only work on the one area you have chosen.

Which category (from the list on the previous pages) should you choose?

- The category in which you find it difficult to use an assertive style.

- The category you *want* to work on.

- The category that causes you the most difficulty, provided that this will not be an overwhelming task.

Your choice: _____

Now for the exercise. For one week, decide to make a priority the one area of nonverbal behavior you have chosen. Which week will you do this? Why not start now?

From: _____   Until: _____

When you catch yourself behaving passively or aggressively, deliberately adopt a more assertive style. For example, if you ordinarily dress to be invisible (a passive style), then each day for a week choose clothing that will make you stand out (bright socks, clothing a little more or less dressy than you usually wear, the tie or scarf that you have been avoiding). If you normally slouch and look away when talking to people, deliberately pull your shoulders back and maintain better eye contact during conversations.

Your old style is automatic, so you will find yourself lapsing back into it. You will have to keep reminding yourself of your task. Do this at least once a day. Here are a few strategies to help you remember to practice:

- If you are working on speaking louder, put a sticky note at your work station with the word "VOLUME" written on it.

- If you are trying to use a more relaxed facial expression, tape a picture of a relaxed person (or the word "RELAX") to your mirror.

- If you want to dress differently, put a reminder on your closet door.

- Wear an elastic band around your wrist.

- Wear your watch on the opposite wrist.

- Wear a ring on a different finger than usual.

Whenever you notice your reminder, go back to practicing the aspect of assertive behavior that you have chosen.

Practice Session: A Walk in Town

This exercise is designed to help you work on certain aspects of your nonverbal style without having to worry about your voice tone. Instead, you will be able to concentrate entirely on your posture, eye contact, and facial expression.

Your task is to go for a fifteen- to thirty-minute walk in a safe public place that is frequented by a lot of people whom you don't know. You may want to walk downtown, in a shopping district, in a park, or in a mall.

When you begin your walk, concentrate on presenting yourself in a confident, comfortable manner. It does not matter if you don't *feel* particularly confident or comfortable. Just walk *as though* you felt this way. If it helps, imagine that you are a particularly confident person you know or have seen on television or in the movies. You can be like an actor, assuming the role of a confident, assertive person. Here are some strategies:

- Walk with an erect posture, your body upright rather than slouched, and your shoulders back.

- Hold your head up and keep your gaze at eye level most of the time, rather than staring at the ground.

- Hold your head directly above your shoulders rather than low and forward (the latter is common to the passive, aggressive, and passive-aggressive styles). Your chest should enter a room before your nose does.

- Maintain a relaxed, easy pace. Allow your arms to swing naturally.

- Adopt a pleasant, friendly expression. See if you can maintain a very slight smile.

- Make brief eye contact with the people you pass. If you look away, glance to the right or left rather than downward.

- Walk in the middle of the path or sidewalk rather than off to one side. When passing others, avoid stepping too far out of the way (as though you were invisible and had to take complete responsibility for avoiding a collision).

- Not difficult enough? Add a smile to the eye contact. Try saying *"hello"* to a few people as you pass.

Monitor how you feel while you are walking this way. It may feel a bit unnatural. After you have gone a few blocks, allow yourself to slouch, avoid eye contact, and assume a fixed, blank expression. Watch the ground. Walk far to one side of the sidewalk, as though you have no right to be there. Monitor how you feel as you walk this way. Perhaps it will feel more natural to you, especially if it is familiar. Perhaps it will feel less confident.

Then, after a few more blocks, change back. Gradually raise your head, loosen up, move your shoulders and head back, and begin making eye contact again. Notice the differences. Continue walking this way for the rest of your walk.

In the weeks ahead, try to catch yourself walking in a nonassertive manner and switch to a more assertive stance.

Practice Session: Working with Your Voice

This exercise is designed to help you work on nonverbal aspects of your voice. You will be using the telephone, so you don't have to worry about your posture, your distance from the other person, the direction you face, or any other aspect of your body position. Instead, you will be able to concentrate entirely on your voice.

Your task is to call someone you don't know and ask for information. Here are some suggestions:

- Call a local hotel and ask for their room prices.

- Call a restaurant and ask whether you would need reservations for a party of four on a Saturday evening.

- Call the library and ask whether they have a "books on tape" collection and, if so, for how long tapes may be borrowed.

- Call a ticket agency and ask about the availability of good seats for an upcoming performance.

- Call a shop from which you have recently received a flyer; ask about the availability of one of the items listed on their promotional material.

During your call, do not be too concerned about the actual words you use. At this point you are mainly working on the other qualities of your voice. Following are some suggestions that might ease this exercise for you.

- Before dialing, place your hand over your stomach. Breathe slowly and deeply using your diaphragm for a minute or two. Your stomach should expand each time you breathe in and relax each time you breathe out.

- Rehearse what you want to say so that you will be able to say it as calmly and evenly as you can, without rushing or hesitating.

- Make an effort to speak loudly enough for the other person to hear. Continue to breathe using your stomach. Attempt to speak "from the diaphragm" rather than "from the head."

- Use a warm, conversational tone. Avoid apologizing, excusing yourself, or (at the other end of the scale) sounding aggressive or hostile. Avoid moving into an angry or impatient mode even if the person answering is slow, awkward, impatient, or doesn't know the answer to your question. Try to keep your tone friendly and conversational.

When you are done, notice whether your mind automatically slips into self-criticism. Perhaps you will catch yourself saying (or thinking) one of the following:

- *"I wasn't clear enough."*

- *"I should have done that better."*

- *"I'll never be able to do this right."*

- *"I've humiliated myself."*

- What else? _____

Gently remind yourself that this is only an exercise; that perfection is neither expected nor desired. Also remember that it doesn't matter what the person you spoke with thinks about you, since they don't know who you are. Repeat the exercise at least twice.

Partner Exercise: Nonverbal Rehearsal Face-to-Face

If you are working with a partner, this is an exercise you can carry out together. If you are working alone, you can do the exercise by addressing yourself in the mirror. The object is to practice the nonverbal aspects of the assertive style in a structured situation and to receive feedback on how you are doing (either from your partner or by watching yourself in the mirror). You can use this information when you work on your communication style in everyday life.

Part One: Scripted Rehearsal

In the first part of the exercise you will read (or, even better, recite) a very brief script to yourself or your partner. Here are the instructions:

1. If you are working with a partner, decide who will go first.

2. Choose a brief script from the list below. Try to memorize most or all of the words so that you can recite it without reading constantly from the page.

3. Recite the script to your mirror image or to your partner. Be as natural as possible, as though you were speaking spontaneously to that person

(e.g., pretending that the other person is the shopkeeper, airline attendant, or taxi driver).

4. Use the assertive nonverbal style. Focus your efforts on the particular aspect of the assertive style that gives you the most trouble (eye contact, vocal tone, facial expression, etc.).

5. If you have a partner, ask them to give you feedback on your nonverbal behavior. The person giving the feedback should focus on the positive as well as the negative. What did you do well? What could be improved? If you don't have a partner, critique your own performance. Take note of what you already do well.

6. Act out the scene again, keeping the feedback in mind.

7. Evaluate your second attempt or receive feedback about it from your partner.

8. If you have a partner, switch roles and repeat the exercise.

9. Continue until you have used all of the scripts on the list below.

Scripts

- *"I bought this book here yesterday, and I noticed that there are thirty pages missing. I'd like to get another copy or a refund."*

- *"I'd like to have these pants dry-cleaned, but it's only worth it to me if you can get this spot out completely."*

- *"Excuse me. My friend and I would like to move to a table in a quieter part of the restaurant."*

- *"Hi. My flight was cancelled due to the snowstorm. I'd like to be booked on the next available plane."*

- *"I have nothing to declare, but I would like some assistance with this heavy suitcase. Could you find someone to help me?"*

- *"Excuse me, but I think I'm next in line."*

- *"I'd like to go to the center of town, please. I notice that you haven't started the taxi meter. I'd prefer it to be used."*

- *"My room is quite chilly and the thermostat doesn't seem to be working. Could you send someone up to check it?"*

Part Two: Unscripted Rehearsal

This exercise is similar to the one above but adds an element of improvisation. As before, you will act out a short one-sided scene, either with your partner or with your own image in the mirror. This time, however, you will have to come up with your own words.

The sequence is the same as before. If you have a partner, decide who will go first. Pick a situation from the list of topics below and act it out, improvising your own words. Don't make it longer than a few lines. Either critique your own performance or ask your partner to do it. Remember to take note of both positive and negative elements. Then repeat the task and evaluate your performance again. Continue until you have used all of the topics listed below.

Topics

- Your travel agency has booked you a flight, but you want them to check for a cheaper airfare.

- You want to know if the bus you are on passes the post office before or after the city park.

- You want to see a menu before being seated in a restaurant.

- You would like your physician's receptionist to look for a more convenient appointment time.

- You want a police officer to determine whether the car that struck yours was stolen.

- You would like the key shop to recut a faulty key at no extra charge.

- You want to know from the ticket seller whether the show is likely to sell out tonight.

- You would like to ask the greengrocer whether the produce is grown locally.

- You want to know whether the floor tile comes in a green that would match your coat.

CHAPTER 8

BEING PRESENT: GIVING
YOUR OPINION

To be assertive is to participate in the events of your own life and the lives of others. Part of "being there" is being willing to reveal your attitudes, preferences, ideas, goals, and opinions. We can avoid being open about these things, but in the process, we avoid living our own lives.

It may be difficult to think of all of the situations in which you could give your opinion. Perhaps you have been holding back so long that people no longer ask very often. Perhaps you give your opinion using such an aggressive style that they don't dare ask. But there are thousands of these situations. Here are just a few:

- *Which restaurant do you want to go to tonight?*

- *What did you think of the movie?*

- *We need to decide on the kitchen repairs. What should we do first?*

- *I need your professional opinion on this.*

- *Where should we go on vacation?*

- *Our readers are welcome to write letters to the editor about this article.*

- *How should we handle our daughter's habit of stealing?*

- *What's your view on the death penalty?*

- *Let me tell you this joke about (racial group) . . .*

- *Who are you going to vote for?*

- *Do you mind if I take this?*

- *We're thinking of firing James. What do you think?*

- *Here's a draft of the memo I'm writing. Any thoughts?*

- *Maybe we should get married.*

- *Your grading has to be done by Monday.*

- *So what do you think? Am I ready for an ocean dive?*

You are guaranteed to find yourself in at least some of these or similar situations. Being able to give your opinion in a candid, nonaggressive manner is a necessity.

Think back over the past three days. List three situations in which you could have offered your opinion. Perhaps you did so. Perhaps you held back. Perhaps you expressed your opinion in such a way that others felt they had no room to disagree. Perhaps you expressed it in a roundabout or sarcastic fashion. No matter. Write down the first three you think of.

1. _____

_____

_____

2. _____

_____

_____

3. _____

_____

_____

Many people have difficulty expressing their views openly. Read over the descriptions below. Place a checkmark beside the one that fits you best in most situations. Use the situations you listed above as a rough guide.

☐ **Passive:** You avoid giving your opinion on issues, whether they are minor (*"Did you like the movie?"*) or major (*"Do you think we should end this relationship?"*). You wait for others to give their opinion first. Perhaps you are willing to give your own opinion, but only if you happen to agree with them. Or perhaps you pretend to agree or actually change your own views to suit the other person.

☐ **Aggressive:** You are perfectly willing to give your opinion, but you speak as though to hold any other view is stupid or bad. *"How could you think that?!"* You harshly criticize or make fun of other points of view, whether or not others have revealed how they feel on the issue. If someone does disagree with you, you attempt to change their opinion through intimidation, sarcasm, or heated argument.

☐ **Passive-Aggressive:** You avoid disagreeing with others directly but express strongly opinionated views when you secretly know that others present may be hurt by them. If challenged, you deny knowing that the other person was the target. *"Frank Smythe is the most corrupt politician we've ever had. No, I didn't know you were his campaign manager."* You frequently express views about others who are not present. *"I think Bob is completely out to lunch on this one, don't you?"* You use sarcasm frequently, but rarely directly, and deny negative intent. *"No, I didn't mean anything by it. What do you mean?"*

☐ **Assertive:** You are willing to express your opinion whether or not others have done so. You take ownership of your opinion (*"My own view is . . ."*) rather than presenting it as the only view a reasonable person would take. If someone disagrees you are willing to discuss the issue, but you don't necessarily feel that your mission is to change their mind. You are willing to change your own mind if others provide new information that you hadn't considered, but you don't change your mind just because others think differently.

Like most people, you probably use all four styles at different times. Regardless of which style you checked, it may be helpful for you to practice offering your opinion more openly. Here are some tips:

- **Relax before you start.** You will be able to think more clearly and express yourself better if you are calm. Breathe slowly and deeply as you think about what you want to say. You may wish to use the diaphragmatic breathing exercise presented in chapter 2. Keep your body relaxed as you give your message.

- **Rehearse.** Briefly go over what you plan to say before you say it. Try to word your message clearly. Although ideally you might wish to respond unrehearsed most of the time, coming up with an alternative to your usual style may take a bit of practice. Eventually, the words will come more easily and spontaneously to you.

- **Don't signal a lack of confidence.** Perhaps your mind is not entirely closed. You might be willing to change your opinion in the face of new information. Nevertheless, avoid signaling a feeling of inferiority about the issue. *"I could be completely wrong about this—and you can tell me if I am—but I have sort of been thinking that. . . ."* If you are undecided, say so. If you feel strongly, say so. But don't undermine your own opinion out of the fear that others may disagree.

- **Feel free to signal your openness to other views.** Sometimes you may wish to indicate that although you have an opinion, you are willing to entertain other ideas. *"I don't have a strong preference, but I'd like to try a seafood restaurant."*

- **Own your message.** When offering your opinion, use an "I" statement to show that you take responsibility for your view. *"My own feeling on* *abortion is that. . . ."* When we feel a lack of confidence, it is tempting to appeal to authorities. *"The Surgeon General says. . . ."* Perhaps you imagine that the people to whom you are speaking will be less willing to disagree with the authority than they would be with you. If they do disagree, they will be contesting the authority's position, not yours. You can just step out of the way and pretend that you were just reporting what the authority said, not expressing your opinion at all. *"Don't blame me, that's what he said."* This is dishonest. If it is your view, say so. Own it. Later on you might be willing to give reasons for your opinion (which might involve authorities), but it is still *your* opinion. In the initial statement it is appropriate to acknowledge this. *"I'm opposed to clear-cutting old-growth forests."*

- **Don't apologize for having an opinion.** Apologies are appropriate when you have overstepped your rights. You have a right to have an opinion, so you don't have to apologize for it. Avoid saying things like *"Forgive me for saying this . . ."* or *"I'm really sorry, but I think. . . ."* Is it true that you regret having a point of view?

- **You are not the source of all truth.** It is possible to word one's opinion in a way that crowds others offstage and implies that they have no right to disagree. *"Any thinking person would agree that. . . ."* *"That political party is completely corrupt."* Of course, people do have the right to disagree with you—and to be as annoyingly correct or misguided as you have sometimes been. Avoid wording your opinion as though there is no other way to see the issue.

- **Don't intimidate.** If anyone changes their mind it should be for good reasons, not because you push them until they give in. Don't raise your voice, tower over the other person, stare, threaten (*"What would the boss think if she heard you . . ."*), make a personal attack (*"You're just soft"*), or use guilt (*"Sure, don't care about me . . ."*). Even if you do convince people to agree with you this way, they will only agree until you leave the room. Few people really change their minds due to intimidation.

- **Consider before justifying.** Some people feel threatened when others disagree or challenge their opinions. Then they become angry and go to extraordinary lengths to convince the other person to come around to their own view. This behavior often stems from one of two beliefs: 1) To keep my opinion the other person must share it; if they don't share it I have to change. 2) The worth or validity of my opinion (or me as a person) depends on my ability to defend the position. These beliefs place you in the powerless position of having to change someone else's mind. The other person has all the control. If someone challenges your opinion, you can choose whether or not to defend it. You do not have to convince them that you are right in order to keep your opinion. It is possible simply to acknowledge that you differ. *"I can see that you don't agree."* *"Sounds like you believe _____ and I believe _____ ."* *"No, I'm not going to argue the point, I was simply saying how I feel."*

- **Don't let it slide.** We don't have to give our opinion *every* time an opportunity arises. Sometimes, however, your opinion may not be asked for, but it may be important for you to give anyway. When someone makes a racist comment, tells a tasteless joke, or behaves badly toward someone, you can calmly express your own view. *"Actually, I don't find AIDS jokes funny."* *" I think it's fine that he did it that way."* *"I believe that hitting a child is inappropriate."* *"John, I know you haven't asked, but I feel strongly that adopting a bear cub is a mistake."*

Checkpoint: Offering Your Opinions

Take a look at the list of three situations you came up with a few pages back. Pick one in which you would like to have been more assertive. Make a brief note of it below. If you didn't do the exercise or if you were assertive in all of the situations, think of a recent situation in which you weren't very assertive about offering your opinion. What was it?

_____

_____

_____

What could you have said that would have been more assertive? It may be easier to think of this now that you're not really in the situation.

_____

_____

_____

Is there a situation coming up in the next week in which you would like to express your opinion in a more assertive manner than usual? What is the situation?

_____

_____

_____

Write down a sample assertive statement that you could use to express your opinion in that situation. Take your time and use the tips given above.

_____

_____

_____

Consider putting your plan into action when the situation arises. For at least the coming week, try to become aware of every time that you avoid voicing your opinion or give it in an aggressive manner. Use Assertiveness Scorecards (blank samples are at the back of the book) to keep track of these situations. Make an effort to move gradually toward an assertive, open, nonaggressive style. Reward yourself for your efforts. Forgive yourself for feeling nervous or not getting it quite right. Remind yourself that every new skill requires time and practice.

Practice Session: The Opinion Exchange

This exercise is intended to help you develop your ability to voice your opinion when the situation calls for it. If you are working with a partner, you can do the exercise together. Decide who will go first. If you are working on your own, address yourself in the mirror. Here's your task:

Speaker

- Select an issue from the "Issues List" on page 101 or create your own.

- Think about your opinion on this issue. If you don't have an opinion, make one up.

- You may present your real opinion or an opinion that you don't really hold.

- If you present a false opinion, don't tell your partner that it is false. Try to convince your partner that you really feel this way.

- Your goal is to present your point of view clearly (neither passively nor aggressively). Your goal is *not* to get your partner's approval, nor is it to change your partner's mind or to convince your partner that you are right.

- Take one to two minutes to present your opinion.

Observer (If Working with a Partner)

- Listen attentively to the speaker.

- Avoid nodding, smiling, or showing agreement or disagreement. Your speaker should not know whether you agree.

- When the speaker is finished, provide feedback. Use the checklist on the next page. Start with positive feedback. End with *one or two* suggestions for improvement (even if this means holding back other suggestions).

Evaluation (If Working Alone)

- Look at the checklist of opinion-giving skills below. Evaluate your performance. Consider both the positive and the negative aspects of your opinion giving.

- Decide on one or two aspects of the presentation that could be improved.

Repetition (Alone or with a Partner)

- Repeat the presentation of the opinion, keeping the ideas for improvement in mind.

- Try to maintain an emphasis on improving in those areas.

When Done

- Switch roles (if working with a partner) and repeat.

- Carry out the exercise with at least one or two more issues.

Checklist of Opinion-Giving Skills

☐ Body posture, movement, distance, eye contact, facial expression.

☐ Voice tone, volume, fluency.

☐ Question talking (*"I think it's wrong? It shouldn't happen? I'm against it?"*—passive).

☐ Apologizing (*"I'm sorry, but I really think . . . "*—passive).

☐ Focusing on your own ignorance (*"I don't really know, but . . ."* —passive).

☐ "I" statements (*"I believe that . . ."*—assertive).

☐ Dismissal of other views (*"No one but an idiot would think . . ."* —aggressive or passive-aggressive).

☐ Appeals to authority (*"Research shows . . ."* or *"Experts agree that . . ."* —usually aggressive).

☐ "Of course" statements (*"Obviously . . ."*—assumes agreement; usually aggressive or passive-aggressive).

Issues List

- Preservation of the environment versus resource industry jobs.

- Should public television and radio be government funded?

- Which political party is the best?

- Should fishing be managed federally or locally?

- Should professional sports teams receive tax breaks?

- Are the Olympics corrupt?

- Should pulp mills be forced to clean up discharges into the ocean?

- Should Western countries ever use nuclear weapons first?

- Should Western countries dispose of all nuclear weapons one-sidedly?

- Should business be allowed to invest in countries with poor human rights records?

- Should we ban clothes made by child labor?

- Is child labor justifiable in very poor countries?

- Should panhandlers be forced off the street?

- Should your province or state separate from the country?

- Should young offenders be jailed?

- Should the legal blood alcohol limit for driving be zero?

- Should pornography be censored?

- Is the Internet a good thing?

- Should human cloning be allowed?

- Is sex education in the schools a good idea?

- Do most kids know enough/too much/too little about sex?

- Is the use of photo radar to catch traffic violations a good idea?

- Is graduated driver's licensing a good idea?

- Where is the best place to live in your country?

- Should cultural industries (films, book publishing) be exempt from international trade agreements?

- Who was your country's greatest leader?

- Who was your country's poorest leader?

- Should those who get lost in the woods have to pay for their rescue?

- Should your country participate more or less often in foreign peace-keeping missions?

- Do we need more public housing?

- Do we need more land set aside for wilderness parks?

- Should we have the death penalty?

- Is whaling ever defensible?

CHAPTER 9

TAKING THE GOOD: RECEIVING POSITIVE FEEDBACK

The following four chapters focus on the giving of feedback from one person to another. But why have four chapters on feedback? Why is it so important?

Imagine that you are learning to use scuba equipment. You have your gear on. Your task is to go to the bottom of the pool and pull off your mask to experience water flooding in against your face.

"Do I take the regulator out of my mouth to do it?"

Your instructor looks at you blankly.

"Do I have my gear on right?"

Silence.

"What was I doing wrong last time, when I panicked?"

No response.

"There, how was that?"

Not even a glance.

"Do you think I'm ready for the ocean?"

A shrug.

"Am I doing anything that will get me killed?"

Nothing.

Imagine a world without feedback from others. No one helps you learn anything. No one tells you that you're doing well. No one offers to report on your performance. You end your presentations and the audience stares blankly, as though you are on television a thousand miles away. Your boss refuses to tell you what she thinks of your work. Your partner just looks at you when you ask how the relationship is going.

Nightmarish.

We need feedback from others. Sometimes we can't see what we're doing. *"Did my racquet get high enough on that last serve?"* Sometimes we don't know how to judge the situation. *"How many clients do most people see in a day?"* Sometimes we can't tell whether our actions are having the desired effect. *"Did standing up help, or did I look too threatening?"*

We especially depend on feedback in social situations. Most of us find it difficult to judge our own social behavior. Because we cannot see ourselves as we really are, we often don't know whether we are behaving appropriately or not. One of the main ways that we see ourselves is by receiving feedback from others. They can be our eyes and ears. For example:

- *"Your voice is a bit loud for this theatre."*

- *"You look kind of timid today."*

- *"You have a thread stuck to your shirt."*

- *"You were too hard on her."*

- *"That was nice of you to say."*

We can use feedback from others to adjust our behavior. Of course, we wouldn't want to base our entire lives on the opinions or demands of others, but it can be helpful to know what they see when they look our way. Other people, however, don't always see us very clearly. Their judgments of us are flawed. These flaws come from a number of sources. Here are a few:

- Guesses about what we were thinking or feeling or meaning to do— guesses that are often wrong. *"You really wanted to hurt his feelings." "You were anxious about that meeting." "You just thought I was trying to control you again."*

- Hopes or fears about how we will act. *"You want to have an affair, don't you?" "You secretly love me." "You don't trust me."*

- Overestimates of their own influence on our behavior. *"You forgot your lines because I was in the audience, right?" "You were doing that to impress me." "You're depressed because I got mad at you last week."*

- Unrealistic ideas about appropriate behavior. *"It was rude of you not to invite him on our holiday." "When someone gives their opinion, you should never tell them you disagree." "If you love me, then you should know what I feel without my telling you."*

- A desire to control us with their feedback. *"Next time, I'll expect you to go along with me." "Prove that you love me." "If you talk about that again I'll leave."*

- A desire to hurt us. *"You are an inconsiderate pig." "Your presentation stank." "I'm surprised you never learned better lovemaking skills."*

- A tendency to give vague and unhelpful feedback. *"You should know better." "I thought it went OK." "Some things I liked, others I didn't."*

Given these problems, it can be tempting to ignore outside feedback altogether and never to offer our own feedback to others. But feedback is unavoidable. Consider:

- *"Here's your performance evaluation."*

- *"Please fill out the feedback form."*

- *"You passed that section of the course."*

- *"How do I look?"*

- *"What did you think of the movie I picked?"*

- *"Was it good for you?"*

- *"Did the shirt fit?"*

- *"Do I get the job?"*

- *"Will you marry me?"*

- *"Does this suit me?"*

- *"Did I do the right thing?"*

- *"Do you like my fiancée?"*

- *"Why are you angry?"*

We all find ourselves in many of these situations. Our jobs, our pay rates, our relationships, our personal hygiene, and our health may all depend on various forms of feedback. Further, without feedback, our own behavior can become steadily worse. Think of these examples:

- The boss who never receives negative feedback and, as a result, just becomes more demanding and unreasonable.

- The spouse who never realizes that their behavior is driving their partner crazy.

- The political leader who forbids criticism and becomes steadily more abusive.

- The child who is never told that their behavior is unacceptable and, as a result, becomes spoiled and self-centered.

How can we work with feedback from others that is so often faulty? How do we avoid being crushed by their criticism? How can we find the useful information among the insults? How do we accept their compliments without insulting them? How do we provide feedback to others that is useful?

Let's begin with a discussion of positive feedback, which is often easier to give and receive than is negative feedback. In many situations, positive feedback is a more effective tool for communication, performance improvements, and behavior change. As we shall see in chapter 11, however, negative feedback is also important.

Accepting Positive Feedback

Many people find it hard to accept compliments. This is especially true of people who are not very assertive. Instead, compliments get cast aside. Let's consider how this happens, why it happens, and what the effects of this behavior might be.

How Are Compliments Not Accepted?

Compliments get tossed in the wastebasket in a number of ways. Here are a few.

Ignoring

The person may ignore the compliment altogether, pretending that it was not heard.

Compliment: *"That hat looks good on you."*

Response: *"Where do you want to eat lunch?"*

Or, the remark may not be recognized as a compliment.

Compliment: *"I'd like you to head the new department."*

Response: *"Don't you like the work I'm doing in my current position?"*

Denial

The person may void the compliment by contradicting it.

Compliment: *"You look great today."*

Response: *"No, I don't. I look awful."*

Arguing

The receiver may argue with the person giving the compliment to show that the compliment was misplaced.

Compliment: *"Your project really turned out well."*

Response: *"Nah. The attendance was lower than I projected, we didn't make as much money as we could have, and the elephant was too fat."*

Joking

The receiver may joke with the other person, failing to fully receive the compliment in the way it was meant.

Compliment: *"Listen, I really appreciate the help that you gave me when my mother was so sick."*

Response: *"Oh right, like I had anything better to do!"*

Self-Insult

The receiver may try to balance the positive feedback with self-imposed insults.

Compliment: *"You made great time on that last hill."*

Response: *"I guess it wasn't too bad for a fat old guy."*

Questioning

The receiver questions the judgment of the giver.

Compliment: *"You sang beautifully."*

Response: *"Why would you think that? You must be deaf."*

Narrowing

The receiver accepts a smaller version of the compliment than was intended.

Compliment: *"You look terrific."*

Response: *"It's these socks my sister gave me."*

Boomerang

The receiver quickly returns the compliment.

Compliment: *"You were funny tonight."*

Response: *"You, on the other hand, are hilarious every night."*

Why Are Compliments Not Accepted?

- Many people have been taught that it is conceited to accept a compliment. They think that compliments should always be treated like hot potatoes and should be gotten rid of as soon as possible.

- Some people feel the need to restore balance. A compliment is a positive, so to balance it out they have to devalue the compliment (eliminate the positive), insult themselves (balance it with a negative), or give the other person a compliment in return (positive for positive).

- Some people fear that accepting a compliment will leave them in debt to the other person. The only way to avoid the debt is to get rid of or repay the compliment.

- Many people have a low self-image. Compliments don't fit this image, so these people don't know what to do with them. They think there must be some other explanation for the positive impression they have made (perhaps luck, or good lighting, or the sheer stupidity of the person offering the compliment).

- Some people worry about the motives behind the compliment. As a result, they respond suspiciously and negatively. *"Why did she say that?"* They wonder if they are being set up and forget that simply accepting a compliment does not give others power.

What Is the Effect of Avoiding Compliments?

Some people think that avoiding compliments makes them look good. Perhaps others will see them as modest, down-to-earth, or kind. In reality, declining a compliment is an insult to the person offering it. It suggests that they have bad judgment or that their opinions don't matter to you. As a result, the person giving the compliment may feel awkward, uncomfortable, stupid, or frustrated. And they will probably be less likely to compliment you in the future.

Fending off compliments will probably affect your own mood as well. You are likely to feel worse after the exchange rather than better.

Do you know anyone who routinely denies or tosses back compliments? Who?

_____

When they respond in this way to compliments you give them, what do you think? How do you feel?

_____

_____

_____

The Alternative

The alternative is simply to accept the compliment. Let it in. Thank the person offering the compliment—and do so without narrowing it down, without apologizing, and without returning it immediately. A simple *"thank you"* will do.

It is not arrogant to accept a compliment. It is polite. It tells the giver that you value and appreciate their opinion. Here are some examples:

- *"Thank you."*

- *"Thanks. I worked hard on it."*

- *"I'm glad you liked it."*

- *"Thanks. I appreciate the fact that you noticed."*

- *"Thanks. I feel good about it too."*

Key point: A compliment is a gift to be accepted. It is not a bomb needing to be defused, nor a volleyball needing to be returned.

Practice Session: Accepting Compliments

Practice accepting compliments using the list provided below. If you are working with a partner, take turns offering each other compliments from the list. Feel free to add your own. Don't worry about whether the compliments are realistic. If you are working alone, imagine that someone is giving you the feedback from the list. Then respond.

When you are giving positive feedback, be as open and genuine as you can. If you wish, change some of the wording to fit your usual way of speaking. Try to catch your partner using any of the unaccepting responses. Point these out.

When you are the receiver, accept the compliment as openly as you can. Speak clearly and monitor your nonverbal behavior. Speak directly to the giver and use good posture and eye contact. Notice the feelings that emerge as you accept the compliments. Initially you may feel embarrassed, ashamed, or guilty, as though you are doing something bad, conceited, or impolite. With practice, you may begin to notice a positive, confidence-building feeling in response to the compliments.

When you have practiced with a few of the compliments below, make several that actually apply to your partner.

Samples of Positive Feedback

- *"You landed the plane perfectly."*
- *"You did a great job on that project."*
- *"Did you choose that paint yourself? It looks wonderful!"*
- *"This soup is delicious."*
- *"The computer you set up is working exactly the way I want it to."*
- *"I really like your shirt."*
- *"You look terrific today."*
- *"You're really efficient."*
- *"This is a great piece of work."*
- *"I really like your idea."*
- *"You made an excellent point in the meeting today."*
- *"It was so nice of you to drive me to the clinic."*
- *"I couldn't have made the arrangements without your help."*
- *"You did really well with that."*
- *"You are extremely talented."*
- *"What a great haircut!"*

Practice Session: A Week of Acceptance

For the next week, watch out for any compliments or positive feedback that come your way. Make an effort to accept compliments without downplaying them. Notice how it feels to do this. Accepting positive feedback may feel odd or unnatural at first. Keep at it.

If you find yourself not accepting a compliment, make a note of what you said in response. Use the Assertiveness Scorecards at the back of this book to keep track of your responses. At the end of the week, come back to this page. Compare your nonaccepting responses with the "How are compliments not accepted?" list a few pages back. Are there one or two ways that you usually discard compliments? If so, what are they?

_____

_____

How did people react when you rejected or downplayed their positive feedback?

_____

_____

How did they react when you gave a more accepting response?

_____

_____

What did you feel when you accepted positive feedback? Guilt? Shame? Contentment? Anxiety? Did you notice any effect on how you felt about yourself? Don't get your hopes too high and don't be disappointed—it can take time to learn to allow compliments to raise your self-esteem.

_____

_____

What would be a more accepting response for each of the situations in which you initially failed to accept positive feedback openly?

_____

_____

_____

For the following week, try to catch yourself *before* you discard any compliments and use a more accepting response instead.

CHAPTER 10

GIVING HELPFUL POSITIVE FEEDBACK

You might think that a person who overuses the passive style would have no great difficulty giving positive feedback. They might be giving it constantly, using a *"Here's a compliment, don't attack me"* strategy. In fact, the reverse seems to be true. Most passive individuals not only avoid conflict, they also avoid the expression of positive feeling. They seldom give compliments, express affection, or provide positive feedback. And, of course, the aggressive and passive-aggressive styles don't typically involve giving much praise either.

What about you? Consider the three types of nonassertive behavior. Place a checkmark beside the one that traps you the most often.

☐ **The Passive Style.** If the passive style is your favorite, you may not take the initiative required to express positive feelings. You may also believe that others wouldn't really care what you think anyway.

☐ **The Aggressive Style.** The aggressive style is competitive. Your mission is to get ahead of the other person. Expressing positive feelings or providing compliments may make you feel as though you are handing the advantage to others.

☐ **The Passive-Aggressive Style.** The agenda of the passive-aggressive style is to bring others down, not to raise them up. Positive feedback is designed to do the reverse, and, as a result, you may avoid giving it.

Why Give Positive Feedback?

Why is giving positive feedback so important? There are a number of reasons. Here are a few:

- Compliments, the expression of affection, and the acknowledgment of our efforts are some of the vital benefits of human relationships. If we never provide these, we are missing out on an important role in family, friendships, and work relationships.

- People enjoy being around those who build them up and who sincerely appreciate their good points. Providing positive feedback helps maintain and build our relationships.

- Reward is much more effective than punishment. If we want to encourage changes in someone's behavior, we are more likely to succeed by focusing on their positive actions than by criticizing their negative behavior.

- Positive feedback (*"Yes, you're doing that correctly."*) is essential in the learning of new skills. In all of our instructor roles (teacher, supervisor, coach, parent, mentor), positive feedback is essential to helping others learn.

What Holds Us Back?

A number of factors can prevent us from providing positive feedback to the people around us. Which ones apply to you? Place a checkmark beside the explanations that fit your behavior at least some of the time.

- ☐ **A focus on the negative.** You only notice the behavior of others when you don't like it. When people are acting positively you think there is nothing to discuss. If this describes you, then it would be a good idea to become more aware of what you *do* like and to strive to recognize and acknowledge it when it happens.

- ☐ **Nothing meets the standard**. You have a firm idea of what you expect from someone, and their behavior never reaches that minimum standard. For example, you may expect your child to keep his room at a certain minimum level of tidiness. He might spend some time cleaning it, but if it doesn't meet your standard, you feel reluctant to give him praise. Rather than comparing the outcome to your standard, you may need to compare it to the alternative: an even *messier* room. Praise the progress. This technique is more likely to help you reach the ultimate goal than waiting for it to happen all by itself.

- ☐ **Not knowing what to say.** If you seldom give compliments it can feel awkward and unnatural to start doing so. This problem requires 1) practicing compliments, perhaps in role plays or in front of a mirror, and 2) tolerating the feeling of awkwardness until it fades.

☐ **Fear of 'losing.'** If you have an aggressive style, you are in competition with others. Giving compliments can make you feel as though you are working for the other team. The reality is that most relationships work much better if the competition is dropped.

☐ **Fear of widening the gap.** Low self-esteem can make you feel inferior to others. It can seem as though giving others compliments raises them even higher above you than they are already. The goal: Raise them higher anyway. Tolerate the anxiety. Far from widening the gap, this usually makes the other person feel better toward you, and playing a positive role can make you feel better about yourself.

☐ **Fear of not counting.** If you think little of your own judgment, you may imagine that others don't really care about your opinions or that they would think it strange if you were to compliment them. *"Why would I care what you think of my work?"* As a result you keep quiet. In fact, positive feedback is almost always appreciated.

☐ **They should do it without my support.** You believe that compliments should be reserved for special circumstances and that regularly expected behavior should not be commented on. *"He shouldn't have to be thanked for doing the dishes; that's his job!"* The worry is that complimenting expected behavior would put you in debt to the person. This is based on a false assumption. We thank the person who passes the salt when we ask, even though we expect them to do so. Thanks, praise, and compliments do not put us in debt to others; they support and encourage the behavior we like.

Recommendations

Positive feedback works well and should be provided. Look for opportunities to offer praise and do so. Be honest in your compliments, however:

- **Refrain from the false compliment whenever possible**. *"Oh, Joan, that hot pink wallpaper looks lovely in your kitchen!" "I thought your book about industrial zoning policy was just thrilling—I couldn't put it down!"*

- **Avoid the backhanded compliment, which hides a fist in a velvet glove.** *"Your new hairdo looks so much better; not nearly so mousy as before." "Your report was surprisingly good, based on your past work." "Thank you for cleaning the car; glad you could get around to it at last."*

- **Compliment behavior that has already occurred.** *"Thanks for driving me to the store. Your new car is great." "Thank you for being so agreeable yesterday."* But don't use compliments as a tool to manipulate others in the future. *"Your new car looks terrific! What a coincidence, I just happen to need a ride to the store." "You're so wonderfully agreeable. I have something to ask you. . . ."*

- **Be specific.** When giving positive feedback about a task well done, be as specific as you can. This is especially important if you are supervising the person doing the job. *"I especially like the fact that you cleaned the* *cylinders on the machine; most people miss that."* This tells the person exactly what to repeat next time and lets them know you have paid close attention to their efforts (much more than if you simply said, *"Oh, yes, overall that was very good"*).

- **Use shaping.** Shaping is a learning tool in which you reward gradual approximations to the goal. When teaching someone to swim, for example, you might at first praise them just for getting in the water, even though they're not swimming yet. Then you might praise them for dog-paddling the width of the pool. Eventually, you may compliment them when they learn to breathe properly while doing the crawl. If you withheld your praise until they were swimming perfectly, they would never learn. Offer compliments and positive feedback for improvements and positive behavior; don't withhold praise until the behavior reaches your standard.

Practice Session: Trading Compliments

If you are working with a partner, practice giving and receiving compliments. At first, feel free to give completely unrealistic compliments that don't really apply to your partner. *"Hey, good choice in yachts!" "Your article on particle physics was extremely well worded."* Use the list from the chapter 9 Practice Session entitled "Accepting Compliments." Get feedback from your partner on your style. While you're at it, watch your partner to see whether the feedback is rejected. If it is, refer your partner back to chapter 9 to revisit their style of accepting compliments.

As you get more comfortable, allow yourself to try out some genuine compliments that really apply to the person. *"Thanks for making that comment in the group today—it really cleared some things up for me." "Your feedback on my tendency to look away when talking to people has been really helpful."*

If you are practicing on your own, stand in front of a mirror. Imagine a variety of different people in your life. Practice giving genuine compliments or positive feedback as though they were persent.

Practice Session: Adopting A New Positive Feedback Policy

Each of the following exercises involves adopting a new personal policy on giving positive feedback. It is an excellent idea to do at least one of them. If giving positive feedback is difficult for you, do two or all three of the exercises.

The Daily Compliment Policy

For one week, give at least one compliment or bit of positive feedback per day. It should be one that you would not ordinarily give. You can give it to anyone you choose: salesperson, waitperson, family member, coworker—whomever you wish.

Keep a record of each compliment using the Assertiveness Scorecards at the back of the book. At the end of the week, return to this page and answer these questions:

To whom did you give your compliments? Were they mostly strangers or were they people you know?

_____

Why them? (If it was because they were easier, consider doing the exercise again with a harder group.)

_____

_____

How did you feel as you were giving the compliments?

_____

_____

Did it become easier or harder to give positive feedback over the course of the week? Did it feel different as you went on?

_____

_____

Whether or not it got easier, resolve to continue with the new policy for at least a month. This may seem artificial. It is. You're doing it as an exercise, not as a natural and spontaneous impulse. Over time, however, you may find that giving positive feedback comes easier and you seem to mean it more. You may also begin to notice a gradual shift in the way you normally relate to people—and in the way they relate to you.

The Stranger Policy

Is it hard for you to give positive feedback to people you don't know (such as salespeople, waiters or waitresses, clerks, or bus drivers)? If so, consider adopting the stranger policy. Every time you get reasonable service or can find something positive in the way you have been treated, mention it. Do this for a week.

If you are quick to criticize but slow to praise, shift the ratio of positive to negative feedback.

Currently, do you give more positive feedback (thank you letters, reports of exceptional service, comments on positive experiences) or more negative feedback (letters of complaint, glares, reports of bad service) to strangers who serve you? What do you think is your ratio of positive to negative feedback (for example, one compliment for every four complaints)?

_____

_____

If you give more negative than positive feedback, it may seem that you are perfectly justified: that the service you receive is usually terrible and only occasionally becomes tolerable. You are, of course, within your rights to give any feedback you wish. But the question is this: What do you wish for? If you really want improvements, notice and comment on the good (or the better than usual); don't wait for the perfect.

Make an agreement with yourself that you will change the ratio of positive to negative. If you currently give one positive for every ten negatives, decide to offer at least one positive comment for every two negatives. If you haven't found something positive to say about someone today, then you are not *allowed* to comment on anything negative—no matter how bad it is. If you can manage a one-to-two ratio already, then make it one positive for every negative, or two positives for every negative. What will your ratio be? (Don't get too ambitious here; this exercise is harder than you think!)

_____

Keep this ratio for at least a week. If you have a hard time keeping track, carry paper and a pen with you (or use Assertiveness Scorecards). Make a note each time you compliment someone on their work. Only permit yourself a piece of negative feedback once you have given the right number of compliments. When a week has passed, return to this page.

Were you able to keep to the ratio you picked?

_____

If not, what were the barriers?

_____

_____

When you have been working on this for a while, consider changing your ratio. If you didn't meet your target, then make the ratio a bit easier. If you did achieve your goal, then make it a bit harder. Don't eliminate negative feedback entirely. In fact, don't go much beyond three positives for every negative. Negative feedback is also useful and should not be avoided. But in chapter 12 we will try to make it *constructive* feedback.

What will your new ratio be? Select a ratio that you can maintain for about a month.

_____

That One Relationship

Pick a difficult relationship in your life—someone to whom you have a hard time talking. Maybe you have to nag them to do chores. Maybe you catch yourself criticizing them a lot (constructively or otherwise). Maybe you exchange outright insults or snappish comments. This person might be a spouse, child, parent, other family member, coworker, roommate, or friend. If you have such a relationship, who is the person? (If you have a lot of them, just pick one.)

_____

Right now, how much straightforward positive feedback do you give them? Check one:

□ None

□ Very rarely

□ Weekly

□ Daily

□ More than once a day

For at least a week, give that person *at least* one positive remark each day. If you already give a lot of negative feedback, try to reduce the number of negative remarks at the same time. If you would like this person to change some aspect of their behavior, make a positive comment each time you catch them doing well. Cut back on the negative comments when they are not doing well. Too many children, for example, only get comments when they *don't* do their homework, never when they *do*. Gradually increase the number of positive statements in this relationship. Watch what happens to the person's behavior (but don't expect miracles to appear quickly).

What is your goal for providing feedback to this person for the coming week? Be specific!

_____

_____

After a week: Were you able to keep to your strategy? What was the hardest aspect of changing your usual style? Was anything easier than expected?

_____

_____

_____

_____

What was the outcome for the other person? Did you notice any shift in their behavior? Don't expect too much here: a week is generally too short for much change to occur.

_____

_____

Were there any other changes? Did you get along better or worse than usual? Did this seem related to your change in feedback strategy? How?

_____

_____

_____

Based on this experience, is there anything you would like to change about your strategy in providing feedback to this person? Do you want to continue the current plan or alter it?

_____

_____

_____

Regardless of the exercise(s) you choose to do, keep working on your skill at providing positive feedback. It takes time for this to become a natural, spontaneous response on your part—and probably all of us could improve in this area. It also takes time to realize whether we are sabotaging our positive feedback by being sarcastic or joking when we should be serious or by giving false or backhanded compliments. As we weed these problems out, the benefits of being a source of supportive feedback begin to multiply.

CHAPTER 11

TAKING THE VALUABLE: RECEIVING NEGATIVE FEEDBACK

It can be hard enough to hear what others like about us. Hearing what they don't like, what offended them, what disappointed them, what they thought was silly or beneath us—this can be almost unbearable. The task is made worse by the fact that most of the people in our lives haven't read this book! The "corrective" feedback we receive is often aggressive, vague, and designed for purposes other than to help us out.

Most of us don't like to be criticized. Criticism is almost unavoidable, however. The only way to live a life without criticism is to hide away in a cave and never see anyone. If you are around other people, sooner or later you're going to receive some negative feedback.

Good. We all *need* negative feedback now and then. It's hard for us to see ourselves. We often can't tell how we appear to the rest of the world. We don't know whether our messages are coming across or are having their intended impact. Feedback can help us to understand how we look from the outside. Then we can decide whether to change our behavior so that our actions match our intentions. Feedback from others is like a mirror, showing us to ourselves. Just as we might not like to have a bathroom without a mirror, it would be a bad idea to live a life without feedback from others.

Although this is all very well, there is a problem. Unlike a good mirror, criticism often gives us an inaccurate picture. The negative feedback can be distorted. Some of the factors that can distort it are as follows:

- **Mood**. Sometimes the criticism has more to do with the other person's emotional state than anything about us. The "feedback" is just a form of emotional expression and contains relatively little useful information.

  John: (after hitting his thumb with a hammer) *Hurry up and give me the plywood. You're too slow!*

- **Unrealistic standards**. Some people expect us to be perfect. When we turn out to be merely human, they get angry and let us know that we're not living up to their expectations. Of course, *no one* could live up to their expectations, so this revelation isn't all that helpful.

  Boss: *Joanne, I expected that project review on my desk by now! You've had almost an hour to do it!*

- **Control maneuvers**. Sometimes the person criticizing us secretly wants to control our behavior. If they say we're not doing a good enough job, they feel entitled to seize control. The negative feedback is just a preface to a power grab.

  Keri: *Raoul, this place stinks. You are so lousy at picking vacation spots. From now on I'll plan where we go.*

- **Jealousy**. When you feel inadequate, criticism is one way to bring other people down to your level. Your critic may feel jealous of you and may be trying to restore the balance. Their feedback may tell you that they're jealous, but it tells you little about your own behavior.

  Donald:*Sure, you got to be president of the company, but only because you stabbed everyone else in the back.*

- **Competition**. When someone is competing with you they may want to impair your confidence or performance. If they can slow you down enough, they might win. Negative feedback can be a competitive tactic.

  Marta: *Congratulations on getting your thesis done ahead of me, Scott. If I were you, I'd rewrite the introduction, though.*
  I thought it was pretty weak.

- **Frustration**. Many people hold back negative criticism until they are just about bursting. At that point, their anger and frustration make the message an unhelpful one. They lose the ability to think and express themselves clearly and all you receive is an emotional smack.

  Terry: (suddenly, after an hour of silence in the car) *I can't stand it any more! Pull over! I'm going to drive!*

- **Fear**. Some people are so hesitant to criticize that the feedback comes in a very disguised form, or they may beat around the bush before coming to the point. You may have to wait hours for the real information, or it might never come at all.

  Martin: *Your presentation? Oh, ah, I thought it was good, just ... great really, I kind of thought it went over really well ... there was just this tiny ... well, nothing really, hardly worth mentioning, I mean everything else was so good, it's just, how can I put it, well*

> *... I didn't want to say anything before your lecture in case it threw you off, but ... your fly has been down the whole day.*

Forms of Criticism

As we discovered above, much of the negative feedback we get can be hard to figure out. Responding to it can be even harder. Let's take a look at some of the different types of criticism and the effects they can have on us. Then we'll look at the skills we can use to deal with criticism.

Nonverbal Criticism

Sometimes criticism comes without any words at all. People simply frown, look away, look disgusted, roll their eyes, tap their fingers impatiently, or walk away. Nothing is said. If they *do* talk, they don't bring up the criticism. The only cue you have that they are displeased is their nonverbal behavior.

This is a very powerful form of communication. The person can communicate disapproval but doesn't have to take responsibility. After all, they haven't criticized you! *"What do you mean? I didn't say anything!"* The key here is *deniability*. The person can deny feeling or thinking anything in particular. Meanwhile, they can make you feel anxious and insulted. This is a classic passive-aggressive strategy.

Nonverbal criticism is often designed to control your behavior. By nonverbally communicating disapproval, people may be able to make you agree with them, drop a request, leave them alone, cook them dinner, or give in to their demands. Because they haven't actually asked you for anything, they may feel that they don't owe you anything in return. After all, you changed your mind (or went along with them, or chose a movie they wanted to see, or voted their way, or worked more overtime) on your own. They didn't actually *ask* you to work more overtime. You volunteered. They owe you nothing.

Nonverbal criticism can leave you feeling angry, unappreciated, anxious, and frustrated. You may also feel uncertain about the nature of the message and how to deal with it. *"Is her behavior really directed at me?"* *"Am I making this up?"*

Does anyone in your life give you a lot of nonverbal criticism? Who?

_____

Make a brief note of one situation in which you were given some nonverbal criticism (from the person listed above or someone else). What did you do?

_____

_____

_____

Keep this situation in mind as you read this chapter's sections on reactions and skills.

Indirect Criticism

Indirect criticism is similar to nonverbal criticism, except that some aspect of it appears in what the person actually *says*. It can appear in several forms.

One form is the backhanded compliment. This looks like a positive, well-meant remark on the surface but contains a poison pill at its heart.

- *"Stripes look good on you—they're so slimming."*

- *"How brave of you to do a presentation on a topic you're so unfamiliar with."*

- *"I love your innocent and unsophisticated approach to art."*

- *"Your project actually worked reasonably well, despite everything."*

With indirect criticism, the positive aspect of the compliment depends on a negative assumption. In the examples above: You're fat, you were unprepared, you're ignorant about art, and there were many flaws in your presentation.

Another form is the "innocent" observation. Here the person makes a negative remark about something in general without referring directly to you—but it really is meant as a personal attack.

- *"Depression just seems like a sign of a weak character, don't you think?"*

- *"Doctors are scum—oh, wait, you're a doctor, aren't you?"*

- *"People who vote for that party are idiots."*

- *"That kind of car is only bought to impress people. Oh, it's yours?"*

The hurtfulness of the remark reaches you, but the person can deny ever meaning to include you in the remark. *"Oh, I didn't know you'd had depression." "Oh, no, I just mean doctors in general, not you specifically." "I was speaking at a theoretical level."* They can even use the opportunity to get in a second jab: *"My, you're awfully touchy about this. Anything the matter?"*

Indirect criticism, like nonverbal criticism, is often passive-aggressive. The person performs an aggressive act without having to take responsibility for it.

In your life, who gives you indirect criticism the most often?

_____

Make a brief note of one such situation and how you responded.

_____

_____

_____

Refer back to this situation as you review the section on common reactions to criticism later in this chapter.

Hostile Criticism

In the case of hostile criticism the "feedback" is encased in aggression. Unlike most nonverbal and indirect criticism, the aggressive content is obvious and open. People may invade your personal space, tower over you, assume an aggressive posture, increase the volume of their voice, and attempt to stare you down. In terms of content, the criticism is likely to be:

- Directed at *you* rather than at your behavior. *"You're incompetent"* rather than *"You made a mistake."*

- Exaggerated and absolute. *"You never get anything right."*

- Designed to hurt you rather than to communicate. *"You're a terrible parent"*—where the title "parent" is chosen specifically because it is so important to you.

Where or who does hostile criticism come from most often in your life?

_____

Think of a reasonably recent example, including your reaction.

_____

_____

_____

Think of this situation as you consider the strategies for dealing with criticism explored later in this chapter.

Direct Criticism

Here the criticism is open and direct without being particularly aggressive.

- *"You made a mistake on the Johnson report."*

- *"These dishes aren't washed properly."*

- *"You're making too many demands on me."*

- *"You have to be more productive."*

- *"I don't like your attitude."*

Sometimes direct criticism is properly assertive. Sometimes it has an aggressive element, is too emotional, is too general to be useful, is inaccurate, or betrays an unreasonable expectation. Although it is usually less difficult to deal with than the types of criticism discussed above, it still may not be easy.

Name two people in your life whose negative feedback toward you is usually quite direct.

1. _____

2. _____

Describe a recent situation in which you were given direct criticism. Evaluate it. Was it assertive, aggressive, passive, or passive-aggressive? Direct criticism can be any of these.

_____

_____

_____

Consider your reaction to this situation (and how you might like to change it) as you read the next section.

Reactions to Criticism

Many of the ways that we react to criticism are understandable but can be counterproductive. Here are some of the most common responses. Note that many of these are related and that we often react in more than one unhelpful way to the same criticism.

- **Fear**. This is a normal response to criticism. Sometimes the fear is due to the comment itself (for example, a fear that we really can't do our job properly). Sometimes fear is due to the person's manner. *"He looks so angry—is he going to hit me?"* Sometimes—perhaps most often—our fear is due to what we think the criticism means. *"Does this mean I will lose my job?" "Will my children turn out badly?" "Does she still like me?" "Will I ever get this right?"* Although fear is a perfectly normal emotion, it is worth examining what you are afraid of, exactly. Then evaluate whether the fear is really justified.

- **Anger**. One of the most common emotional responses to being threatened is anger. *"How dare he say that to me?" "As if she has no faults of her own."* Again, the emotion is not really a problem. It can, however, distract us from examining the message (*"Maybe I could do this better"*), and it may make us react in unhelpful ways.

- **Counterattack**. When someone attacks us (and we often think of criticism as an attack), the impulse is to attack back. We even feel justified in attacking: *"They did it first. I'm entitled to my anger."* Rather than ending the conflict, however, this usually just makes it worse. Couples who have conflict problems typically get into patterns in which they trigger one another with minor criticisms that escalate into full-scale war. *"I was perfectly justified in bringing that up, after what he said first."* When was the last time you ever resolved an issue this way?

- **Denial**. It's tempting to respond to criticism with a flat denial. *"Nonsense, I'm a perfectly good parent!" "I don't make mistakes like that."* This looks assertive, and, in some circumstances, it can actually be a viable response. The problem is that denial often has a veiled counterattack hidden inside it: *"You're wrong. You just can't see the situation properly."* True or not, the other person will feel attacked and will likely come back with another criticism. Flat denial often sparks a back-and-forth escalation.

- **Defense**. It's so tempting to defend ourselves. In some circumstances, saying something in our own defense is appropriate. Self-defense, however, often puts the other person into the position of judge and jury over us. *"But I wasn't too bad yesterday, was I?"* *"It's not that messy; besides, I was just about to clean it up."* *"No, no, the reason I did that was ____ and ____ and ____."* Once you have offered your defense, who has the power? The other person does, because they determine whether your defense is good enough. *"I'm still not satisfied with your explanation. Squirm some more for me."* Defending ourselves actually invites this type of response because it implies that you are willing to have them pass judgment on your behavior.

- **Shame and inadequacy**. All of us have a hidden suspicion that we really aren't very adequate or capable human beings. We develop this in early childhood (hopefully along with an opposing sense that we *are* adequate). Criticism can wake up this sleeping suspicion and make us feel terrible about ourselves. Although this is normal, it can interfere with our ability to respond in a useful way to negative feedback. Rather than wallowing in shame and self-loathing, we may actually want to think through the feedback. *"OK, so I misfiled something. How could I organize things better the next time?"* *"Hmm, he got angry with me just after hitting himself with the hammer—maybe his remark was not about me so much as a reaction to his own frustration."*

Skills for Coping with Criticism

Think of a recent situation in which you received some negative feedback and the exchange went poorly. Perhaps you got angry and attacked. Perhaps you said nothing and wish you had been more effective. Perhaps the other person seemed to feel invited to elaborate on the negative aspects of your performance at great length. Who were you dealing with?

_____

What was the situation?

_____

_____

There are various strategies for dealing with negative feedback from others. Keep the situation you have identified in mind as you read over the following tips. Place a checkmark beside each idea that may have been useful to remember in that particular situation or others you have faced recently.

☐ **Relax**. Criticism may cause you to tense up. This will put you into a defensive or aggressive body posture, change the emotional tone of your voice, and make it harder to think of an effective response. Before you respond to a criticism, relax yourself as much as you can by breathing deeply and slowly, unclenching your hands, and releasing the tension in your face and body.

☐ **Avoid retaliation**. Don't immediately turn the focus onto the other person. *"Oh yeah? Well, you left your muddy boots on the carpet yesterday!"* This tempting gambit makes the other person feel they haven't been heard, and they will usually either become angry or repeat the negative feedback more forcefully and less helpfully. Stay with the topic—even if you know that the other person is vulnerable on a related issue.

☐ **Hold back**. The intention of some indirect criticism is to "get a rise out of you." In other words, the person *wants* you to get upset about the remark so they can deny any negative intentions. *"Boy, are you ever touchy! I didn't mean anything by it!"* Then they can feel free to criticize you even more. *"You really need to calm down. No one can tell you anything!"* An alternative strategy is simply to ignore the nasty face or the offensive comment. This isn't always the best thing to do with indirect criticism. It can be a good idea, though, when the intention is clearly to get you to retaliate.

☐ **Consider your safety**. Some critical people are physically violent. This is especially a concern when you know that the person has been violent in the past or when the person confronting you is a stranger. Averting violence is more important than coming up with the best assertive response, so exercise caution in these exchanges.

☐ **Don't demand perfection**. Most people aren't all that great at providing negative feedback. One option is to demand that every bit of feedback they give you should be phrased in exactly the right way, otherwise you won't pay any attention to it. Unfortunately, this will rob you of some good opportunities to learn from feedback you receive. Even when some feedback is not expressed well, consider whether there may be some value in it.

☐ **Validate their perception**. If you can see why they might think the way they do, say so. *"I can see how you'd think that."* This defuses some of the frustration and makes a reasonable exchange more likely. The fear holding you back from doing this is usually a belief that the other person will feel they have "won." The reality is that they usually calm down enough to have a sane discussion.

☐ **Validate their emotions**. If the person is upset, acknowledge this. *"You're really concerned about this." "I can see that this has upset you."* The person will usually feel that they have been heard and will relax. Some of the emotional drama you see is designed to show you that it's a serious issue. If you signal that you have received the message, the function of the emotion has been served and the emotional display may subside. Then you can talk more easily.

☐ **Agree in part**. Sometimes you may be unwilling to agree with the entire criticism. *"Yes, Dr. Welby, I am the most inept surgical nurse who ever lived."* But you may genuinely agree with a part of the criticism. If so, it can be wise to let your critic know this. *"You're right, my suturing isn't as good as I'd like it to be."* *"You're right, I do have failings as a mother."* The specific point (your suturing skills) may have been what they meant all along. The exaggeration (*"You're completely incompetent"*) was just the usual lack of precision that people use when giving negative feedback. Once you have the real topic on the table, you can have an open and honest discussion. *"You're right, I do make mistakes."*

☐ **Listen and wait**. Before you respond, allow critics to voice their points completely. Listen. Eventually they will slow down and be more prepared for an open exchange. If you jump in with your response too quickly, they will feel blocked and their emotional tone will usually escalate. Listening to criticism does not mean that you have to buy it or believe it. You take the criticism *in*, but you don't necessarily take it *on*.

☐ **Narrow and specify**. People are often vague when they provide criticism. It can seem as though they are critiquing everything about you (*"You're a complete idiot"*) when, in reality, they are just reacting to a single event (*"You cut off that truck back there"*). Ask what the criticism is really about—without jabbing them too hard for being imprecise. *"You seem really upset. Could you tell me when you felt I was being inconsiderate?"* *"You know, I do make mistakes. Which one are you most concerned about right now?"*

☐ **Ask for clarification**. When you are given indirect or nonverbal criticism, it's fair to ask the person about it. Rather than responding to what you *guess* they mean, ask them. This forces the person to take responsibility for the criticism. If they say, *"Stockbrokers all live only for money,"* you might reply, *"I'm a stockbroker. I'm not sure what you mean."* In response to a dirty look, you might say, *"I'm not sure what that expression meant."* If the person refuses to elaborate, that is their right. You cannot control their behavior and you cannot force them to be open. You have communicated, however, that you will not respond to communication for which the person will not take responsibility.

☐ **Explain without offering excuses**. If appropriate, you may wish to offer your version of events with a *brief* explanation. *"Oh, I'm sorry I missed that call—it was my day off."* *"You're right, I did forget that—I was very busy Tuesday."* Do not go on at length, however. *"I know I forgot to call you on your birthday, but ___ and ___ and ___ and ___ happened, and then ___ and then. . . ."* Long strings of excuses communicate a lack of confidence and invite your critic to challenge you.

☐ **Don't try to change their mind**. You can't control what others think. They have a right to their opinions—even if they are mistaken. If you try to force them to change, you hand them power. Don't keep justifying, explaining, and arguing endlessly until they agree with you. They may *never* agree with you. They don't have to, and you don't need them to. Even in the odd case when it seems you *do* need them to agree with you (perhaps at work), you can't force them to do so.

☐ **Thank the critic**. As has been repeated several times in this section, we need feedback. When someone gives us something we need, it is appropriate to thank them. Consider thanking them even if you didn't ask for the feedback, even if it wasn't given in a particularly nice style, and even if you have no intention of acting in accordance with their advice. Thanking them makes them feel heard and reminds us that simple feedback doesn't hurt us.

☐ **Respond to the style**. React to the manner in which the criticism is given. If the person is kind and obviously well-meaning, offer some positive feedback on their style. If the criticism was given in an intentionally hurtful way, consider pointing this out to your critic and suggest an alternative way of communicating. *"Thanks for telling me. I usually respond best, though, if you're really specific about what upset you."*

☐ **Ask for time**. Sometimes it may not be appropriate to respond at the time. The other person may be so upset that they will react negatively to anything you say. You may want time to ponder the possible truthfulness of the feedback. It may take you a while to figure out how to respond. If so, consider asking to meet at a later date to clarify what has been said. *"Thanks for going over my performance review. I'd like to meet next week to talk it over once I've had a chance to absorb what you've said."*

In Sum: Examples

Here are some sample responses to a common type of criticism.

Criticism:	*"You've been doing sloppy work and goofing off lately."*
Unhelpful responses:	*"No I haven't. I've been 100 percent organized and productive!"*
	"Well, you aren't such a great worker either."
	"Oh, but I had that dental appointment last week, and then there was the Johnson project, and you remember the fire alarm on Tuesday, and besides, Frank in the next office hasn't finished his part yet."
Better responses:	*"I can understand that you might think that way."*
	"Hmm. Can you give me an example?"
	"What's bothering you the most at the moment?"
	"You're right. I have been a bit sloppy this week."
	"Can you tell me what you'd like me to do differently?"

Go back to the negative feedback situation you identified earlier in this chapter. Based on what you have read, is there anything you would like to have done differently? How would you like to have handled the situation?

The one situation you identified may or may not be representative of the feedback situations you find yourself in most often. Perhaps other situations would require very different responses.

Review the list of coping skills and take note of the ideas beside which you have placed checkmarks. Which two seem most important for you to practice?

1. _____

2. _____

Make use of these strategies in the next exercise.

Checkpoint: Developing Responses to Criticism

Using the tips above, come up with some helpful responses for the following criticisms. The first one is already filled out with a few sample responses.

Criticism: *You're late for your appointment—again.*

Responses: *"You're right."*
                   "You sound upset. What have I missed?"
                   "Yes, I'm sorry about that. Usually I'm more punctual."
                   "Thanks for letting me know."
                   "Yes, I was late last time, wasn't I?"
                   "Yes, that's twice in a row I've been late now."

You never make dinner just right. _____

_____

_____

You're very moody today. _____

_____

_____

You can never commit to a relationship, can you? _____

_____

_____

You're about as stupid as anyone I've ever met. _____

_____

You're going to lose this game for the team unless you smarten up.

_____

_____

_____

You're not very productive. _____

_____

_____

We're going to have an accident unless you slow down and stop driving like an idiot.

_____

_____

_____

You care more about that television than you do about anything else.

_____

_____

_____

Feeling stuck? There's a trap in this exercise and you may have fallen into it. It's the belief that you have to convince the other person that they are wrong about you. This *is* a trap! It's a helpless position. Don't try to convince them. Acknowledge the comment and move on—either to a productive discussion or to another topic.

For example, here are some responses to *"You're about as stupid as anyone I've ever met"*: *"Really?" "You're right, I do some mindless things. What are you thinking of?" "How so?" "You sound really angry at me." "Thanks for letting me know." "I see."* None of these answers falls into the trap of trying to convince critics that they are mistaken, and none gives the flat denial that invites retaliation. Some may be more helpful with strangers, others with friends. But all are better than trying desperately to convince them that you're really not stupid.

Practice Session: Rehearsal for Accepting Criticism

It's a good idea to practice receiving critical feedback in an artificial situation before attempting to cope with real situations. This provides you the opportunity to try out various types of responses to various types of critical feedback.

If you are working with a partner, you can take turns giving and receiving feedback. If you don't have a partner to work with, you can practice responding to imagined criticism.

Take a look at the list of topics below and the descriptions of the different forms of criticism, then read over the exercise instructions that follow.

Topic List

- You did a lousy spacewalk.

- You didn't get the job.

- I'm giving you a low grade on your job performance form.

- I don't like your report on the project.

- The redecorating job on your house isn't to my taste.

- Your artwork is ugly.

- Your room is dirty.

- You're going out too much.

- You talk on the phone too much.

- You're driving the car carelessly.

- I think you're seeing your new boy/girlfriend too much.

- You're not saving enough money from your paycheck.

Types of Negative Feedback

The critic in this exercise can provide feedback using any of the four types of criticism (nonverbal, indirect, hostile, and direct) discussed earlier in the chapter. For more information on each of the types, you may wish to read the section again. If you are conducting the exercise alone, imagine receiving criticism fitting each type.

Each of the different types of feedback lends itself particularly well to one or more of the interaction styles we have been discussing (passive, aggressive, passive-aggressive, and assertive). The person playing the critic can attempt to use any or all of the styles if desired. If the assertive style of providing criticism seems difficult, not to worry. Using this style to give constructive criticism is discussed in the next chapter.

- **Nonverbal criticism.** Choose a topic from the list above. If you are working with a partner, choose the topic together. Ensure that both of you know what the situation is about, since the critic won't be saying much. Decide whether you will be passive, aggressive, or passive-aggressive. Nonverbal criticism lends itself to all three. If you are passive, do everything possible to avoid revealing what you don't like. Look evasive. If the receiver asks, deny that you have any criticism to give. If you are aggressive, convey disapproval by frowns, nasty looks, impatient signals, bored expressions, and hostile silence. If you are passive-aggressive, tone down the hostility while making it clear that you disapprove of something. If the receiver asks what it is, deny everything. Try to keep the receiver guessing, and imply that he or she is overly sensitive.

- **Indirect criticism**. Choose a topic, then word the criticism in an indirect way. This type of feedback suits the passive-aggressive style best. You might give a backhanded compliment: *"Congratulations! I'm amazed you were able to survive that spacewalk given the amount of trouble you usually have with them."* Another technique is the apparently innocent observation that is secretly designed to hurt. *"We decided to give the job to someone who was qualified."* This implies that the listener wasn't.

- **Hostile criticism**. This type of feedback fits the aggressive style most closely. Give the feedback in an aggressive manner with an emphasis on the nonverbal behavior. One option is to be loud, invade the person's personal space, tower over the receiver, angle your body aggressively forward, and glare while making sweeping generalizations. Another strategy is to pull back into hostile, icy withdrawal. Speak quietly but threateningly, be coolly detached, and use words carefully calculated to hurt. Remember, though: This is an exercise, not real criticism. Make sure you pick topics that are not real issues for the two of you.

- **Direct criticism**. This form of feedback can be properly assertive. If you choose this style, be clear, open, and relaxed. Focus on exactly what you mean and convey a continued caring for the individual. Don't worry about getting it just right, however. Direct criticism can also have aggressive or passive elements. Let yourself be a bit too general, too emotional, or too vague. The point here is to give the receiver a chance to respond to feedback that is less than perfect.

The Exercise

If you are on your own, position yourself in front of a mirror so that you will be able to evaluate your performance. You will be both critic and receiver.

If you are working with a partner, decide who will take on the critic role first. Collaborate in selecting a topic and agree on any setup that is necessary. *"OK, I've just gotten back in the spaceship after trying to repair something."* Remember: Don't try to choose a particularly realistic topic at this point. You are practicing with criticisms that don't hit too close to home.

The critic and receiver should jointly agree on a type of feedback to try out. The critic then delivers the feedback in the chosen style.

The receiver responds using the skills described in this chapter, emphasizing those that he or she most wants to practice. The receiver is entitled to call a "time out" to think before responding. (This is one of the benefits of rehearsal, after all.)

The critic can then respond in character or give genuine feedback on how the receiver's reaction would likely come across.

The receiver can try again based on the critic's feedback (though the goal here is not necessarily to satisfy the critic).

Once you have done a few of these artificial situations, you can try one or two that are slightly more realistic, based on people in the receiver's real life. If you ever try situations that involve a genuine issue between the receiver and the critic, make sure 1) that the issue is a very minor one, and 2) that you use a direct and assertive (i.e., nonaggressive) style rather than any of the others. It may be better, however, to hold onto these issues until you have both read the next chapter.

Practice Session: Monitoring and Rewriting Your Responses in Real Life

Sometimes it's hard to come up with the right response on the spot. There isn't much time to think and you may be feeling strong emotions. It's good practice to go back and think about these exchanges later, when you have some time. You may be able to see more clearly what the other person was doing and how you would like to have responded. This exercise encourages you to do just that.

1. For one week, monitor all of the criticisms that you get from other people. Use Assertiveness Scorecards or spare paper.

2. Write down each criticism and who it is from.

3. Write down your response at the time.

4. Evaluate your response. Was it assertive? Was it negative or defensive? What did you do right?

5. Rewrite your response. Come up with a revised answer that may have been better than what you actually said. You don't have to go back to the person and give your new response. It's enough to know what you would like to have said.

Here's an example:

Person/Situation: Boss said *"You're too slow."* I think he's mad I haven't booked his flight yet.

Your Response: *"I'm working as fast as I can! I'll get to it!"*

Assertive, Passive, Aggressive, or P/A?   Angry and defensive. Aggessive

Feelings Afterward: Felt inadequate.

Alternative Response: *"There's a lot on my plate right now. Was there something in particular that you were hoping to get before now?"*

Is there one person in your life who criticizes you a great deal? If so, you might wish to focus your exercise on that person. Who is it?

_____

Keep up the exercise for at least one week. With practice, you should find that you become more aware of your usual style of responding to criticism and how this can be improved. Initially, the more helpful response will only come to you once the situation has passed. Eventually, you should find that you think of and verbalize it on the spot, while you are still in the situation.

CHAPTER 12

CONSTRUCTIVE, NOT CRITICAL: GIVING CORRECTIVE FEEDBACK

Many people find giving negative feedback even more difficult than receiving it. Some are so uncomfortable that they avoid providing negative feedback altogether. The word "negative" may convince you that this is fine. Who needs more negatives in life?

The reality is that negative feedback is essential to all of us. Without it, most relationships are likely to degrade and fall apart. The ability to provide constructive feedback when appropriate is a vital skill in our personal and professional lives. All of us need to give negative feedback now and then. Consider a few examples:

- In supervisory positions it is important to inform those we supervise about mistakes or poor performance. *"Harvey, it's important we get the plans out today."*

- When dealing with supervisors we must be able to state what we can and cannot do, what we are not willing to do, and what problems are arising. *"Our team won't be able to finish that job until Tuesday."*

- In instructional settings, we must be able to point out errors or make suggestions for improvement. *"Margaret, holding the paddle like that will make you tired too quickly. Try lowering it."*

- With children it is our duty to restrain some of their behavior. *"I know you're eager to get to the park, but we always wait for the green light."*

- In romantic relationships, our partners depend on our feedback to know what is and is not OK with us. *"I'm frustrated you didn't tell me you were going to spend an extra day on the trip."*

- Our friends often rely on our honest feedback. *"Why didn't you tell me my dress wasn't done up?"* *"Am I crazy to marry someone with that kind of history?"*

The fact is that some negative feedback (as *negative* as that term may sound) is important in almost all relationships.

The Effects of Discomfort

Our discomfort in providing corrective feedback may cause several problems, each of which pulls us away from effectiveness. The three most common faults are listed below. When you become uncomfortable, one of these reactions may occur more than the others. Try to rank them from one (most troublesome for you) to three (least).

_____ **Avoidance**. You may just avoid giving corrective feedback at all. This is a recipe for disaster in most relationships. Your children will go out of control, your coworkers and employers will not respect you, and your friends may feel betrayed. *"Why didn't you tell me you were feeling that way?"*

_____ **Aggression**. If you are not comfortable giving corrective feedback, you may become angry when you are forced to do so. You may not really be angry with the other person. Instead, you may be angry that you are forced to confront them, which you hate doing. The feedback you give when angry is unlikely to be helpful. *"That's it! Blast it, John, stop ordering my meals for me! You are an overbearing idiot!"*

_____ **Vagueness**. Discomfort giving corrective feedback may cause you to be imprecise when you finally do it. This passive style is unhelpful and usually makes others impatient. *"Well, uh, to tell the truth, uh, the part that I thought wasn't so great was . . . uh, um. . . ."*

Your most common reaction may not be on the list. When the situation calls for corrective feedback and you become uncomfortable, is there something else you do? What is it?

Skills for Providing Corrective Feedback

So how can we make our corrective feedback useful? There are a number of principles, but one stands out. This is the most important one, and the one that is frequently the biggest problem for people:

Key Point: Focus on the behavior, not on the person.

When many people give negative feedback they focus on the person:

- *"You're incompetent."*

- *"You need more self-esteem."*

- *"You're too clumsy."*

- *"You have a bad attitude."*

- *"You're too conservative."*

- *"You're not respectful."*

Each of these statements focuses on an aspect of the person rather than an aspect of their behavior. Why not focus on personality traits? First, the person has little control over these broad, general characteristics. How, exactly, do you change a "bad attitude"? Even if we are right, that the person has a bad attitude, they can only change their behavior. If corrective feedback is to be useful, the person has to be able to change something. If they can't change it, the feedback is pointless. *"I think you need to be more intelligent."* What's the use in this?

Second, focusing on a general characteristic is usually *inaccurate*. When we give feedback, we aren't responding to the person's imaginary and invisible personality traits. We are responding to their *behavior*. If a coworker always hands us work late on a Friday afternoon, what don't we like? It's tempting to say that we hate her lack of consideration. What we are *really* reacting to, however, is receiving work just before the weekend. Our feedback should focus on the behavior that we don't like—not our guess about the *reason* for the behavior. Even if our guess is right (she *is* inconsiderate), she can't change that overnight. What she *can* change, and what bothers us, is her habit of giving us work on Friday afternoons.

Conclusion: When giving negative feedback, always focus on the behavior that you hope the person will change. Don't focus on the reason behind the behavior.

The following is a list of additional skills and strategies that can help you to provide appropriate and helpful corrective feedback. As you read the items, think of the most common problems you have when faced with these situations. Place a checkmark beside those skills that you need to practice.

☐ **Choose your timing**. Don't start giving your feedback when the other person is stressed, distracted, or too rushed to pay close attention to what you have to say. The only reason to give corrective feedback is to help the other person, and it will be no help if they can't focus on your message.

☐ **Watch the ratio**. Remember that positive feedback is more powerful than negative and tends to cement relationships. Ask yourself which type you give more often. If you overdo it on the negative side, then try to increase the amount of positive feedback. What do they do *right*?

☐ **Think before talking**. It's easy to get off track when giving corrective feedback. Before you get started, think through exactly what you want to say and how you will say it. If giving corrective feedback is especially hard for you, you could take some time to make notes on what you'd like to say. You won't want to use notes forever, but they can be a fine tool to help you overcome your reluctance.

☐ **Talk one-to-one**. Avoid giving corrective feedback when there is more than one person present. Most people find it humiliating to be criticized in front of others (though the more supportively and assertively you give the feedback, the less of a problem this is). They will focus more on their own embarrassment than on your message. Instead, try to catch the person alone or invite them to meet with you one-on-one. Don't forget to protect your safety, though. *"Angela, could I meet with you in your office for a moment?"*

☐ **Frame the issue**. If what you say is likely to seem threatening to the person, start out with a clear statement that places a boundary around the issue. *"Your swimming is going really well. On the backstroke, though, your right hand doesn't come up as high as. . . ." "I really enjoy the time we spend together. That's why I want to tell you how I've been reacting to your lateness. . . ."* The frame signals that your criticism is not about a larger issue and doesn't mean that you are rejecting the person completely.

☐ **Be precise**. For feedback to be useful, the person has to know exactly what you are talking about. If you say, *"I didn't like your presentation,"* they will have no idea what to change. Perhaps they should stop giving presentations altogether. However, if you say, *"I couldn't read your handwriting on the board,"* they will know exactly what to do. Be specific and give details.

☐ **Include the positive in the message**. Consider starting your feedback with what you *did* like. This way people won't feel that you are attacking them, and they may be more open to considering your feedback. *"Here's what I thought you did really well . . . and here's what I thought could have been better. . . ."*

☐ **Give information, not advice**. Direct advice is often resisted by those receiving it, and rightly so. People have the right to decide for themselves what they will and will not do. When giving corrective feedback, focus on giving information about the problem. Let the other person decide what to do about it. *"Your shirt has come out"* is better than *"Tuck your shirt in." "I couldn't hear you"* is better than *"Speak up."*

☐ **Don't emote**. When giving corrective feedback you may be feeling powerful negative emotions. *"I can't believe that SOB is handing me even more work!"* Choose what you want to do. Do you want to let off steam, or do you want to provide information that the other person can use?

Don't try to do both. In general, loud expressions of frustration or anger will cause the other person to feel threatened, and clear-headed contemplation of the feedback will go out the window. Sometimes your emotional response to the person's behavior *is* your feedback. Even so, a calm report is often more useful to the person than a heated display. *"I'm feeling frustrated by the workload because I can't get it done as quickly as I would like."*

Some of these ideas you probably already use. Others may seem inappropriate for certain situations in which you find yourself. Which ones seem most likely to be helpful if you were to practice them? Come up with one or two. Ensure that you focus on these in the exercises to follow.

1. _____

2. _____

Checkpoint: Comfort and Skill in Providing Corrective Feedback

Consider your own life. Who are some of the people to whom you might need to give corrective feedback now and then? In this exercise you are asked to name four.

For each person, think of an issue about which you would like to be able to give corrective feedback more effectively.

Rate how *comfortable* you feel giving the person feedback on this issue. Do you get anxious or hostile, or are you relaxed and confident? Use a 0 to 10 scale, where 0 is not at all comfortable and 10 is very comfortable.

Then rate how *effective* you are at giving the feedback on another 0 to 10 scale (where 0 is "completely ineffective" and 10 is "very effective"). Effectiveness means that the person understands exactly what you mean and what you think would be better and doesn't seem to feel personally attacked.

Here's an example:

Person: <u>The senior vice-president of the company.</u>

Issue: <u>Turning in his gas receipts late every month.</u>

Comfort: <u>8 (I feel fine telling him)</u>   Effectiveness: <u>0 (He never seems to get it)</u>

Now try your own:

1. Person: _____

Issue: _____

_____

Comfort (0-10): _____ Effectiveness (0–10): _____

2. Person: _____

Issue: _____

_____

Comfort (0-10): _____ Effectiveness (0–10): _____

3. Person: _____

Issue: _____

_____

Comfort (0-10): _____ Effectiveness (0–10): _____

4. Person: _____

Issue: _____

_____

Comfort (0-10): _____ Effectiveness (0–10): _____

Now, add all four of your comfort scores together: _____

Add all of your effectiveness scores together: _____

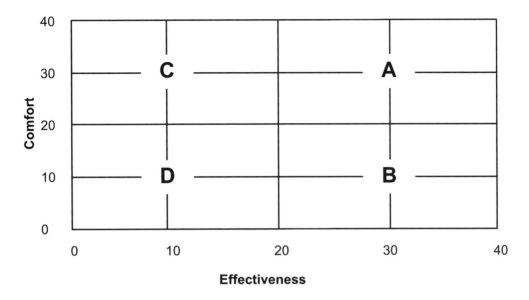

Graph your results on the chart. Notice that your comfort score is represented on the vertical axis, while your effectiveness score is along the horizontal. Mark the place where your scores intersect with an X. For example, if your comfort total was 10 and your effectiveness total was 30, you would place an X over the B. If your comfort total was 30 and your effectiveness total was 10, place an X over the C.

Notice that there are four quadrants on the graph.

Quadrant D

If your scores place you within the quadrant marked D, then you probably see yourself as neither comfortable nor effective at providing constructive feedback. Your discomfort probably distorts the way you give feedback. Perhaps you avoid giving feedback due to anxiety, or the feedback you give is vague and imprecise, or your feedback is given in a hostile manner because you resent having to do it. When it comes to giving feedback, your style is most likely passive or passive-aggressive. It would be a good idea for you to reread chapters 2, 4, and 5 (on stress, negative beliefs about assertiveness, and positive beliefs).

Quadrant C

If your scores place you in the quadrant marked C, then your discomfort is probably not a significant problem. You are not held back by fear. But you still see yourself as being ineffective. This suggests a need to build up your skills at providing corrective feedback. It may be that you provide feedback in a somewhat insensitive way that comes across as aggressive or hurtful, though it may also be that you are overly vague. You may need extra practice with the strategies presented in this section. Another possibility is that you judge yourself as ineffective unless the person receiving your feedback agrees with you or follows your advice. If so, remember that the assertive style involves making your own position clear but allowing others to decide for themselves how they will behave.

Quadrant B

If your scores place you in quadrant B, then you see yourself as being effective, but you still don't like giving constructive feedback. Perhaps you imagine that others will be crushed by your feedback. If they are, then you aren't really all that effective after all. Perhaps you hold back until you are very angry and then burst forth with your criticism in an aggressive way that doesn't help the situation. If the exchange usually goes well, perhaps you could benefit from regular relaxation practice (perhaps diaphragmatic breathing, discussed in chapter 2) just before giving feedback.

Quadrant A

If your scores place you in quadrant A, congratulations. You report that you are both comfortable and effective in most situations involving the provision of constructive feedback. This is the goal. The closer you are to the top right-hand corner of the graph, the more true this is. Of course, you may be mistaken. Perhaps you have forgotten some of your anxiety about giving feedback, or perhaps others would question whether you are as effective as you think you are. Reviewing and practicing the skills in this section will help cement your position in this quadrant or move you even further to the top right.

Checkpoint: Giving Effective Feedback

In this exercise, practice wording your feedback according to the principles given in the list of skills a few pages back. Each example gives the situation and a sample of the aggressive "personal attack" style of corrective feedback. In its place, give a more useful and assertive form of feedback without lapsing into passive avoidance or passive-aggressive manipulation.

Example

- Situation: Franklin is late for work for the fourth time this week.

- Ineffective: *"You don't care about this job enough!"*

- Effective: *"Franklin, the store has to open promptly at 9 a.m. It's not acceptable to be late this often. Let's sit down and discuss the problem."*

Your Turn

- Situation: Carol, age six, has just crossed the street without looking both ways.

- Ineffective: *"You're going to be killed if you don't watch out!"*

- Effective:

_____

_____

- Situation: The boss has just handed you the third major project in a week.

- Ineffective: *"You're unreasonable and too demanding."*

- Effective:

_____

_____

- Situation: Your spouse has not helped tidy your home in a month.

- Ineffective: *"You are a complete and utter slob."*

- Effective:

_____

_____

- Situation: Your best friend has just asked how you liked her terrible overacting in a community theater production.

- Ineffective: *"You seemed to think there wasn't anyone else on stage!"*

- Effective:

_____

_____

Have you been filling out Assertiveness Scorecards (see the Introduction and the back of the book) for yourself as you have been reading this book? If so, and if they frequently reveal problems with the way you give corrective feedback, practice rewriting the feedback you give in real-life situations. Gradually, you should find that you are more able to provide helpful feedback on the spot.

Practice Session: Constructive Feedback Rehearsal

Practice wording and delivering helpful constructive feedback using an assertive style. If you have a partner, one of you can concentrate on giving the feedback while the other can practice receiving it assertively using the skills from the previous chapter. Because the feedback is delivered well, the receiver may find hearing and accepting it quite easy to do.

If you don't have a partner to work with, do mirror practice instead. The main focus of the exercise is on wording the feedback, so a partner isn't really essential.

Begin by choosing a few topics from the list below.

- You feel that your partner is making too many demands on you.

- You suspect that your partner is afraid of commitment in relationships.

- You want to tell your friend that he needs to be more assertive.

- Your car-pool buddy has arrived late to pick you up for the third day in a row.

- Your employee is not working hard enough to justify her salary.

- Your child hasn't finished the chores that were agreed on.

- Your roommate complains that life is dull but just sits around the house all day.

- Your boss is giving you too much work.

- You have received complaints from customers that your checkout person is rude.

- Your lead singer is singing off-key.

Take some time to think about how to word your feedback in an assertive, helpful manner using the skills from this chapter. The nice thing about providing feedback is that you usually have time to think before you do it. Then give the feedback to your partner using appropriate, relaxed, and assertive body language. Repeat this several times using different topics from the list. If you are working with a partner, they can practice their skills at receiving feedback.

Next, try something a bit more realistic. Think of some feedback that you would really like to be able to give someone in your life (*not* your practice partner). Perhaps it is feedback that you have been avoiding giving to the person. Perhaps every time you try to give it, something goes wrong and you wind up in a fight. Have your partner play-act being that person. Think carefully about how you would like to give the feedback (and what you really hope for from the situation). You may find it helpful to write it down. Then try it out on your partner. Get feedback from your partner on your technique, then repeat the exercise again. If you are working alone, give the feedback to the mirror. Imagine how it would be to hear this message.

Next try something that may prove even more instructive. Practice providing feedback about *your own* troublesome traits. If your kitchen is a mess, play the part of a roommate who constructively raises the issue. Keep practicing until you have a way of providing the feedback that you yourself would react well to. (You might not clean your kitchen, but you would be able to hear the feedback without becoming furious or hurt.) If you are working with a partner, see if they agree that the message seems clear and reasonable.

Practice Session: A Week of Feedback

Set aside a week to work on giving constructive feedback. Here are the steps:

1. For one week, become aware of each situation in which you *must* or *could* provide either negative or constructive feedback. To whom do you normally give this kind of feedback? When?

_____

_____

_____

2. Stop yourself before you give the feedback. Ask yourself what you would normally do in this situation. Would your usual response be assertive, passive, or passive-aggressive?

_____

3. Using the suggestions in this section, come up with a way of providing the feedback that would be more constructive or helpful than your usual style. You may have to delay giving the feedback until you have had time to think.

4. Provide the feedback and watch the individual's response. Compare it with their usual response when you have given them feedback in the past. It may be better. It may also be worse than usual, if your technique is unfamiliar to them.

5. Record the exchange using an Assertiveness Scorecard. Write down the situation, what you said, and how the person responded. At the end of the week collect your descriptions and see if you notice any patterns.

Option: Tracking Your Changes

After a period of working on your style of providing feedback, go back to the Checkpoint exercise earlier in this chapter entitled, "Comfort and Skill in Providing Corrective Feedback." Complete the exercise again (with the same people in mind, if appropriate). Graph your outcome again and see if you are any closer to the upper right-hand corner (quadrant A). If so, congratulate yourself and keep working. If not, consider whether you need to change your strategy. Is it the comfort level or the effectiveness that is now the problem? Target your work accordingly.

CHAPTER 13

THE ASSERTIVE "NO"

Ah, saying no. This is the hallmark difficulty of the passive style. Passive people usually have a hard time turning down requests from others. *Any* requests. It doesn't matter how unreasonable they may be.

Why is saying no so important?

Key Point: If you cannot say no, you are not in charge of your own life.

That's it. Period. If others ask you to do something, you have to do it. There is no other choice. In effect, you are a slave. You can't make any of the rules. You can't decide what you will and won't do. The only way you can be left in peace is if others don't ask you to do anything.

But they *will* ask. Of course they will. Who wouldn't? Imagine having a genie who will carry out any request you make. It would be wonderful. If you can't say no, you *are* such a genie for the rest of the world. Once the rest of the world discovers it, they will be unable to resist.

- *"Can I borrow your couch?"*

- *"Will you drive me to the doctor's? I go three times a week."*

- *"Here's some more of my work for you to do."*

- *"You can handle the kids on your own, right?"*

- *"I'm moving this afternoon; can you come and help?"*

- *"I know I'm an adult, but I need someone to take care of me."*

- *"Mom, iron my shirt!"*

- *"Can you write this report and put my name on it?"*

- *"Get this to me by Friday."*

- *"The back forty acres needs harvesting."*

Will you do it? Sure you will. You don't have a choice. You don't believe you're *allowed* to say no. Even if it's inconvenient. Even if it means you get no sleep. Even if it makes your children grow up to be helpless because they've never done anything for themselves. Even if it costs you your peace of mind.

Saying no also poses problems for those who overuse the aggressive and passive-aggressive styles. The anger fueling aggression often comes from a desire that others not ask and a belief that anything less than a hostile blast will be ineffective. As well, saying no involves taking responsibility for the refusal, which the passive-aggressive individual wishes to avoid. The passive-aggressive strategy is to say yes and then fail to go along with the request anyway.

Barriers to Saying No

If saying no is so important, why don't people do it? Why don't you? What holds people back? There are several motivations. Place a checkmark by the reasons that seem particularly fitting in your own case.

- ☐ **Wanting them not to ask.** You shouldn't *have* to say no. If others were more considerate they wouldn't ask you to do so many unreasonable things! This belief may cause you to be resentful and angry. The reality, though, is that others have the right to ask you anything they want. *"Can I have your house?"* And you do have the right to say no—whether or not you use that right.

- ☐ **They won't accept it.** You think that even if you did say no, the people in your life would assume you'd go along with them anyway. You might be right about this. If you have gone along with all of their requests for years, they may expect you to continue in that role. The first few times you say no, they won't really believe what they hear—unless you show you mean it.

- ☐ **They won't accept *me*.** You believe that the only reason anyone accepts you is that you're willing to do all the dirty work. If you stopped doing it, they wouldn't like you or accept you anymore. You'd be alone. It *is* possible that some people only have you in their lives because you play the role of servant. But if so, do you really want these relationships?

- ☐ **I don't have the *right* to say no.** It's selfish to take care of your own needs or to treat yourself as an equal to the others around you. Isn't it? Well, no, it's just a recognition of reality. You do have the right to say no. You do have needs like everyone else, and you are entitled to take care of yourself. Remember that we're not talking about becoming the most selfish person on earth. We're talking about it being your decision what you will and will not do.

Checkpoint: Getting Unreasonable Requests

When do you receive unwelcome requests the most? Is it at work? In a volunteer organization? In a romantic relationship? From relatives? From children? Who usually does the asking?

Do they need to ask, or do they just assume that you'll do things without their asking? *"I'm sure she'll iron my shirts if I leave them here on the floor."* Do they hint around until you volunteer? *"That tree sure needs pruning, doesn't it? I sure wish someone would do it. . . ."*

What kinds of things do they ask for?

Perhaps these are the situations you need to work on. Keep them in mind for the exercises to follow.

Strategies for Saying No

There's nothing wrong with saying yes, doing favors, or taking on responsibilities. Problems arise, though, if you do these things because you can't say no or don't know how to do so. Here are some things to keep in mind for those times when you wish to say no. Place a checkmark beside the skills you most need to practice. Then emphasize the ones you checked when you carry out the exercises at the end of the chapter.

- ☐ **Use assertive body posture.** Use direct eye contact, keep your head up, shoulders back, hands relaxed or gesturing normally, and voice calm and loud enough to be heard. If you communicate "no" with your words and fear or "maybe" with your body, people will believe the message of your body and push harder.

- ☐ **Decide on your position before you speak**. If you're not sure what your answer is, don't answer yet. Decide exactly what you are and are not willing to do. If you're wishy-washy or uncertain, you invite others to push you into a "yes" response. If necessary, ask for a few days to think about it.

- ☐ **Wait for the question.** Some people agree before they are even asked! Here's an example. Distant acquaintance: *"Gosh, I'm not sure how I'm going to get there. . . ."* You: *"Oh, I'll drive you."* If this is one of your stumbling blocks, then even a hint is enough to get you to volunteer your time. This is convenient for the other person because they don't owe you anything—after all, they didn't ask you for the favor, you volunteered. Volunteering is just fine—when you *choose* to do it. But if you find yourself volunteering more than you would like and feeling weighed down by too many of the resulting obligations, force yourself to wait for the request. For one thing, requests tend to be fewer than hints. For another, waiting forces others to take responsibility for their requests. *"Gosh, I'm not sure how I'm going to get there. . . ."* (Silence.) *"Would you mind driving me there?" "OK."* This is one of those interesting occasions in which the assertive thing to do is simply to keep your mouth shut for a while.

☐ **Decide on your wording**. Think through not only *what* you want to say but also *how* you want to say it. Otherwise you are much more likely to stammer, wander about, and invite a challenge. Be clear about your answer. Don't leave your questioner wondering what you really mean. If you mean to say no, don't say, *"I'm not sure if . . ."* or *"Maybe later sometime. . . ."* Instead, word it clearly: *"No, I'm not willing to do that."*

☐ **Don't apologize when it isn't necessary**. Apologies put you in the debt of the person asking you to do something. They suggest that the other person is entitled to expect you to grant the favor. Is that the message you want to give? If not, avoid lines like *"I'm sorry but I really can't . . ."* or *"I really should but. . . ."*

☐ **Don't defend yourself or make excuses when it isn't necessary**. Offering excuses about why you can't fulfill the request is usually dishonest. It's not that you *can't* do it, it's that you *choose* not to do it. Giving excuses also invites the other person to help you find a way around the barrier: *"You can't because you have to have the car serviced? No problem, you can do that tonight at a garage I know, then you'll be free to drive me tomorrow."*

☐ **Don't ask permission to say no**. Remember that you have the right to say no. You don't have to ask permission. If you do ask permission, it tells the other person that they are in charge of your behavior, not you. Wrong message. Avoid saying, *"Would it be okay if I didn't . . ."* or *"Will you be annoyed if I say no?"*

☐ **Strengthen your position**. Don't expect that people will accept your refusal the first time you turn them down—especially if you've been saying yes for years. Be ready for them to push again, and respond with a refusal that is just as strong or stronger. Don't sound like you're weakening. *"No, as I've said, I'm not willing to do that." "Again, I'm not willing to do that." "No."*

☐ **The broken record technique**. Don't feel you have to rephrase your response every time you give it. Doing so may cause the person making the request to believe you are weakening. *"Eventually he'll run out of ways of saying no, then he'll say yes."* You don't have to find the magic words that will satisfy the other person. Using a response once doesn't wear it out. If you keep repeating the same message, eventually they'll hear it. *"No, I'm not willing to do that." "No, I'm not willing to do that."*

"No, I'm not willing to do that." Worried that this will sound odd? Doesn't matter. It won't sound as odd as you think. At any rate, the fear of sounding odd is a trap that can keep you in the control of others.

☐ **Don't wait for acceptance.** You don't have to convince others to accept your refusal or agree with it. *"You don't see why I can't? Let's see if I can explain it better. . . ."* This assumes that you have the right to say no only if you can convince others to see your point. If you keep explaining yourself every time they repeat the request, then you are saying that they have the ultimate power. They don't. You do. *"I can see that you don't agree. Nevertheless, that's my decision."*

☐ **Accept the consequences**. You have the right to say no, but others have the right not to like it. In fact, others are entitled to think you are inconsiderate or unreasonable. Sometimes they may be right. When you say no, there might be unpleasant consequences in the way that others react. Recognize and accept this. Uncle Frank might really be offended if you say he can't stay at your home all next spring. He's allowed to feel whatever he feels.

Case in Point

Kathy, an English as a Second Language instructor at the local community college, was ready to quit her job. She felt burnt out and beset by demands and obligations. Not only did she carry a full teaching load, she also sat on seven different administrative committees, edited an English-language newsletter for the students, and had somehow managed to become a quasi-legal advocate for her students' immigration concerns. Every time there was a crisis people came to her.

Kathy recognized that her usual style was passive. She accepted virtually every request. Lately, however, it was less than clear-cut. In what Kathy suspected was a passive-aggressive fashion, she sometimes neglected to do some of the things she had agreed to do. Several times recently she had exploded at people making demands on her, berating them for always coming to her and never asking anyone else. It was these aggressive outbursts, more than anything else, that had made her question her career. Maybe another work setting wouldn't be so demanding.

While taking an assertiveness course, Kathy came to a realization. Her fantasy of a work environment without excessive demands was just that—a fantasy. Anyone with her style of taking on responsibilities would find herself overloaded in almost any workplace. Her angry outbursts and her passive-aggressive behavior were simply the result of built-up resentment and anxiety at her pile of responsibilities. The problem wasn't the college. The problem was her inability to say no.

Kathy began to practice saying no in front of a mirror, imagining herself faced with some of the requests that had recently been made of her. Initially she felt an overpowering temptation to apologize and offer excuses for her refusals. She painstakingly trimmed down her replies to the imagined demands and practiced repeating her refusals patiently but assertively when she guessed that they would not be accepted at once.

Then she came up with a plan. First, she forbade herself from volunteering her help unless she was asked directly. She realized that she had never actually been asked to perform many of the duties she had taken on—she had simply volunteered her time when someone hinted about a task that needed doing. For the next month, she would wait for the question. Second, she would accept no new duties on the spot. Rather than saying yes immediately, she had to allow herself at least one day to think about any new request. That would give her the time to evaluate whether she really had the energy and interest to go along with the request. Finally, she would forbid herself from taking on any new administrative work—the part of her job she hated the most. She rehearsed saying no with a friend who tried every means possible to extract a yes from her.

The next few weeks were surprising. Every time she refused or put off a request she felt guilt and pressure, but she realized that most of it came from within. As time passed, and as she reminded herself that she had the right to say no, the guilt gradually eased. One colleague congratulated her for finally giving up the role of departmental doormat. Others seemed genuinely confused. Some pushed harder, allowing her a chance to practice repeated refusals. *"Nope, I've decided I'm already doing enough."* A few expressed concern, wondering if she was ill or having family problems.

The experiment also forced Kathy to watch the collapse of one of her secret convictions: that the place would fall apart unless she did everything. Tasks that really needed to be done still got done—sometimes by people Kathy had suspected would never lift a finger. Somehow the atmosphere of her department even seemed to improve. Kathy began to wonder whether her playing mother to everyone else had actually prevented them from participating.

Kathy experienced a hint of disappointment upon realizing that she was not quite as essential as she had imagined. Eventually the sense of pressure began to fade. She gave up some of her administrative work, while still doing what was required, and she kept most of her work on behalf of students, which she actually enjoyed. By reminding herself that she could refuse requests, she began to fear them less. By reminding herself that she had a choice about many of her duties, she began to feel more that her work was her own. She began to enjoy teaching again.

Practice Session: Fending Off Requests

In this exercise you will practice saying no in an assertive manner. If you are working on your own, think of someone you know who is quite pushy. This works best if it is someone to whom you usually feel uncomfortable saying no. Who will you use?

You will be imagining this person making obnoxious requests of you; then you will practice responding assertively to the request—aloud and preferably in front of a mirror so that you can watch your nonverbal behavior.

If you are working with a partner, one of you will play the asker, the other will be the refuser. The asker should choose a request from the list below without consulting with the refuser. After all, one seldom knows what others are going to ask us for, and we should be prepared to deal with the unexpected. The requests may be reasonable or wildly unreasonable (preferably at least one of each).

The asker should make the request without any attempt to be respectfully assertive. Be as pushy as you like. Repeat your request, use guilt, imply that the person owes you a favor, lay the friendship on the line, and take advantage of any other strategy you can think of.

The refuser's job is to decline the request without becoming aggressive.

Either of you can call for a time-out to think and plot your next move if you wish. During time-outs the refuser can enlist the help of the asker if desired. Then get back into the roles.

Repeat the exercise with two or three different requests. The refuser can choose at least one of these requests based on past situations that have proven difficult.

Then consider these questions alone or with your partner.

- **For the refuser**: How easy or difficult was it to refuse? How was it to have the asker keep asking? How did you feel? Guilty, anxious, strong?

- **For the asker**: Was there anything in the refusal that invited you to keep trying? Anything that signaled you could get what you wanted by being pushier? Anything that communicated that the person's mind was or was not made up?

If you have a partner, switch roles and repeat the exercise.

Request List

- I can't make my mortgage payment this month. Can you loan me the money?

- Train me how to do your job.

- I have too much work. Could you handle some of it for me?

- Can I borrow that book you're reading?

- Can I borrow your toothbrush? I forgot mine at home.

- Buy me a drink, would you?

- I need to get on this ferry more than you do. Let me go ahead of you.

- Can I borrow your lawnmower?

- I'd like you to invest in this company I'm starting.

- Give this couch to me at a better price.

- Mom/Dad, I want to go away for the weekend with my boyfriend/girlfriend.

- Sister/Brother, I'd like you to handle all of mom's financial affairs.

- I'd like you to change the date of the office party—I can't make it that night.

- I really want you to hire me instead of that other person.

- Type this up for me, would you?

- But I want to ride to the ski hill in Frank's car. He's had his license since Friday!

- I'd like you to take on the Sarducci account.

- Please review this file and have a report on my desk by 9 AM tomorrow.

- I have too many cats. I'm giving this one to you.

- I'm allergic to paint—could you paint my house for me?

Practice Session: Think before You Agree

Sometimes we agree without even thinking. Someone makes the request and we say *"Sure!"* almost automatically. If saying no is hard for you, you might be automatically saying yes to everything. *"Could you lift that elephant onto this bicycle for me?" "Sure!"*

Before you can say no, you have to stop agreeing automatically. Make a deal with yourself: Before you respond to any request (or any hint of a request), you have to recognize that it *is* a request. For one week, don't agree to anything until you have said to yourself, *"That's a request. I can choose to say yes or no."* Then let yourself respond or put off a response until you have had time to think.

Carry a pen and paper with you for the week. Assertiveness Scorecards (located at the back of the book) will do nicely. Write down any requests that you don't feel completely comfortable about. Make a note of what you did in the situation.

Once you are out of the situation and have some time to think, decide whether you are satisfied with your response. If not, write down a response that you think would have been better.

Try one out now based on your experiences this past week. Briefly describe a request you received and did not really want to agree to. If possible, pick one that you think you did not respond to as well as you would like.

_____

_____

What did you do or say?

_____

_____

What could you have done differently? Try to come up with the words you would like to have used.

_____

_____

_____

Do this same exercise with requests you receive in the coming week.

Optional Practice: Delaying Agreement

Make an agreement with yourself that for one week you will not say yes to any requests or volunteer for any activities until you have had at least a day to think. If people request favors of you, your job is to put them off for at least one day.

"Extra committee work? I'll let you know Monday."

"Your shirts? I'll tell you tomorrow whether I have time to iron them."

This delaying tactic will give you time to a) decide whether you really want to say yes or no, and b) think of how to word your answers.

CHAPTER 14

MAKING REQUESTS WITHOUT
CONTROLLING OTHERS

Being assertive usually means controlling your own behavior without attempting to control the behavior of anyone else. For example, when you say no, you assert your right to decide for yourself what you will and will not do. Setting this boundary can be extremely difficult for the nonassertive person.

The situation becomes more complicated when we make requests of other people. At first glance, it can look like we're trying to control their behavior. *"I want you to fill up my car when you use it."* In reality, though, we are simply stating what we would like to happen. We are informing others of our desires. We leave it up to them to decide whether they will go along with the request. They keep control over their own actions. We retain control over our own actions, including the response we make if they do or do not grant the request. *"Otherwise I will be less willing to loan you the car in future."*

Many people are quite passive when it comes to making requests. They feel they don't have the right to ask for things. *"I can't ask him to fill my own car with gas; that would be rude."* Or they may fear the consequences of the request. *"What if she says no?" "What if they think I was stupid for asking?" "What if I'm being unreasonable?"* The result: Passive individuals commonly avoid asking for help even when it is perfectly reasonable to do so. They hope that others will happen to notice what's needed and provide it. When this doesn't work, they feel resentful and used.

Some people are too aggressive. They feel entitled to control the behavior of others and so assume that their requests will be granted. *"Next time you're going to fill up the car."* They do not make requests so much as demands. *"Get me a beer, would ya?"* If others don't grant the request, or do so poorly or slowly, these individuals become angry. Anger, as we discussed in chapter 2, is a sign of feeling threatened. What's being threatened here is the aggressive individual's delusion that they have control over others.

Still others behave passive-aggressively when they want something. They make neither requests nor demands. Instead, they orchestrate circumstances to force others into doing what they want. *"I know, I'll leave the car almost empty. Then he'll be forced to gas it up." "Honey, I was trying to get another beer for myself, but my knee gave out on me. Gosh, it hurts."* Sometimes this works, though others typically see through the manipulation more easily than the passive-aggressive person imagines. They may be inspired (and feel justified) to get passive-aggressive in return. *"Fill it with seventy-five cents of regular, please." "Sorry, Honey, I can't seem to find the beer."* Further, because the passive-aggressive strategy involves controlling the behavior of others, it ultimately reinforces a sense of helplessness and anxiety.

So how can we become more comfortable making requests? Consider these tips and observations.

- Begin by asking yourself what you would like to happen in the situation. Imagine that you don't have to worry about other people's feelings or rights. (You will want to take their feelings into account before you actually ask, but at this point you need to know what you really want.) If you are used to taking a passive stance, you may find that it's hard to know what you want, let alone to ask for it.

- Then, before making your request, decide for yourself what you think would actually be reasonable, given the circumstances. Try not to underestimate your rights. If you are usually passive, it might feel unforgivably rude to make a perfectly reasonable request. *"No, it would be far too impolite to ask him to stop talking during the symphony."* Reread chapter 5 if you have difficulty deciding what's reasonable.

- Don't apologize for asking. You have the right to ask for just about anything—as long as you recognize that the other person has the right to refuse. Apologizing tells the person, *"I don't really feel like I'm entitled to have you do this for me, but . . . ."*

- Avoid putting yourself down as part of the request. For example, *"Excuse me, but I seem to be too disorganized this morning to find the parking lot. Could you direct me?"* Instead, try to ask in as straightforward a way as possible.

- Word your request as a request, not as a demand. It can be just fine to make a request in a way that seems to presume others will agree—but make sure it is still a request. *"Could I see your license?"* Note that requests do not have to be worded as questions. *"I'd like to have a glass of water, please." "Please gas the car up on the way back."*

Describe, Express, Specify, Outcome Scripts

One way to become more comfortable making requests is to use Describe, Express, Specify, Outcome (DESO) scripts, as proposed by Bower and Bower (1991) in their excellent (and recommended) book *Asserting Yourself*. Describe, express, specify, and outcome are the four steps in making an assertive request. The intent is to frame the situation, say what's wrong, make your request, and predict an outcome. Thinking in terms of DESO scripts makes coming up with a request much easier and makes the request more likely to be heard by the other person.

Let's consider each step in more detail.

Describe

Before making your request, define the situation. What's going on? Be as clear as you can without making a long speech.

- *"There's a lot to do before I can serve dinner."*
- *"It's been a long time since we went out together."*
- *"I noticed that the lawn needs cutting."*
- *"I bought this coffee grinder here yesterday and the cord is missing."*

If your request has to do with someone else's behavior, focus on the behavior rather than on the person's personality or motives.

- Not great: *"You're lazy and inconsiderate."*
- Better: *"You haven't yet done the chore you agreed to do last week."*
- Not great: *"You're paying me so badly because you think you can get away with it."*
- Better: *"I'm not making as much as other people who have this job."*

The behavior of others is less open to argument than their motivation or personality. The chore has either been done or it hasn't. You're either making less than the others or you aren't. It's open to debate whether the chore wasn't done due to laziness or whether the low pay is due to greed on the part of your employer. Your goal is to make a request, not to invite the other person to argue. As well, accusing the person of having a negative personality trait or poor motive is likely to make them defensive, and they will resist the rest of your message. Always focus on the behavior.

Express

This is the second step in your request. Express how you are feeling in this situation. Here are some tips:

- **State your emotions clearly, don't act them out.** Avoid using the Express stage to "let them have it" with the full impact of your emotions. A simple statement will do. *"I'm not feeling valued at the moment."* This can feel like an understatement when what you really want to say is, *"I can't stand it anymore, you selfish jerk!"* But it will usually have a better outcome.

- **Emphasize the positive.** Focus a bit more on the positive emotions you wish you were feeling than on the negative emotions you are currently feeling. Sometimes it is entirely appropriate to say, *"I get very angry when that happens."* But often it can be more helpful to say, *"I don't feel as close to you as I would like."* An emphasis on the positive communicates that you value the relationship and the person but that something (about which you have a request) is getting in the way.

- **Stay calm.** Try to keep a reasonably calm and even tone when you are saying what you feel. You don't have to be as detached as a robot. A simple statement that you feel angry is often more helpful than the same message shouted with bared teeth.

- **Use "I" statements.** Take responsibility for your emotions. You should not be trying to blame how you feel on the other person. This will only make them defensive (*"It's not my fault, it's **yours**!"*) or cause them to feel bad (*"You're right, I'm completely worthless"*). We will never bring out the best in people this way. Using the word "I" shows that you take responsibility for how you feel. *"I'm feeling overwhelmed"* is better than *"No one could stand this"* or *"This is unbearable."* "I" statements make your requests more personal, they communicate that you take responsibility for your own feelings, and they avoid implicit insults (*"Anyone would see that your behavior is unreasonable, you dolt!"*).

- **Avoid martyrdom.** Some people find it tempting to overemphasize how bad they feel in the situation (the "poor me" problem). The hidden agenda is that they want to make the other person feel terribly guilty. *"When you didn't come to my party I just felt worthless, like the whole thing was a complete waste of time."* The hope is that the guilt will make the other person want to change. This usually doesn't work. Even when it does work, it often damages the relationship. State how you feel, but don't overstate it.

Sometimes you can skip the Express stage. If you are asking for directions to the parking lot, for example, you don't have to say how anxious you're feeling.

Specify

This is when you make your request. Specify what you would like to happen. Some tips:

- **Decide what you want ahead of time.** You may feel anxious talking to the person, which will make it harder for you to think on the spot. So before you get started, decide what you want and how you will word the request.

- **Be clear but brief.** In most situations, your request should take no more than one or two sentences. Be specific. Here's a bad example: *"I'd like you to take a more active role on the committee."* What does that mean, exactly? Better: *"I'd like you to handle the fundraising for the next six months."*

- **Frame the request positively.** Say what you want, not what you don't want. *"I'd like the garbage to be taken out by eight o'clock"* is better than *"Don't be so lazy about taking the garbage out."*

- **Focus on behavior.** What do you want the person to *do*? Don't ask for changes in how the person thinks or feels. *"Stop resenting me so much." "Stop being so stubborn." "I'd like you to have a better attitude."* Also avoid being too general. *"I want you to be more considerate."* Each of these is likely to confuse the issue or make the other person resist your request.

Here are some examples of appropriate "specify" statements:

- *"I'd like you to set the table for dinner."*

- *"I want you to be home before midnight."*

- *"When you're feeling angry, I'd like you to write me a note saying what you object to."*

- *"Let's sit down and plan who will pick up the kids each day."*

The more specific you are, the greater the opportunity for the other person to go along with your request.

Outcome

The last step is to describe the outcome that you think will follow if the other person does or does not go along with what you suggest. Bower and Bower refer to this stage as "Consequences." For some people this usually means punishment, and so the word "Outcome" has been substituted here. What kinds of outcomes do we mean?

Feelings

Perhaps you will simply feel better. This may be the most frequent type of outcome statement that you will make.

- *"I'd really like that much better."*

- *"Then I think I would feel more comfortable."*

- *"If you do that, I think I'll be much less overwhelmed."*

Results

Sometimes your outcome will be a concrete effect in the outside world.

- *"I think the project will get done much faster that way, and we can relax sooner."*

- *"That would remove one of the barriers between us, and I think we would get along better."*

- *"Then I would be able to get the most important things done first, and you wouldn't be left waiting."*

- *"I think that would raise your employee rating next time around."*

Reward

Perhaps you will do something for the other person in return.

- *"Then I'll give you a massage when you get home."*

- *"If you do that, I'll take over the laundry this week."*

- *"If so, you can invite a friend over for a movie tomorrow."*

- *"Then you can have the car next Thursday."*

Punishment

Perhaps if the person *doesn't* do what you request, you will do something they won't like. **Note**: You should use this one extremely sparingly (even with children). Most people overuse punishment as a way of getting what they want. Reward is usually much more effective. Sometimes, however, punishment is appropriate:

- *"If the garbage is not out by eight, there will be no television tonight."*

- *"If you aren't able to be faithful to me, I will have to do something I don't want to do: end the relationship."*

- *"If the sexual remarks keep up, I will report them to the human resources department."*

By stating an outcome you once again take responsibility for your own behavior and let others keep responsibility for their behavior. You are not demanding that others do anything. This would be trying to control their behavior. Instead, you are simply saying what you will feel and do if they act in certain ways. Others are invited to consider the situation and decide what to do of their own free will.

Remember that negative consequences often cause resentment. Punishments are less effective at changing behavior than are rewards. In most situations, take some extra time to frame your consequences in a positive way. Consider adopting the "three-to-one policy." This means that you strive to give at least three times as many rewards as punishments and three times as many compliments as criticisms.

One more tip about outcomes: People often make outcome statements that are vague or excessive. These are unlikely to come true. If you do this, others will learn not to take you seriously. Here are some poor outcome statements:

- *"Or I'll ground you for an entire year!"* (Not likely!)

- *"If you don't, boy are you going to get it."* (It? What do you mean?)
- *"Then I'll love you forever, darling."* (Until the next demand, anyway.)
- *"Then everything will work out perfectly!"* (Nothing works perfectly.)

Be specific and realistic when making your outcome statements.

Case Examples

Here are a few examples of complete DESO scripts:

"Ivan, when I arrived at the river I realized that you hadn't sent the paddles on ahead (Describe). I was frustrated because that meant we didn't have enough for everyone to practice with (Express). I'd like you to come up with a plan to ensure that on future trips everything gets packed and sent, and then run it past me (Specify). That way, I can feel more confident taking people out there and I won't be hassling you afterward (Outcome)."

"Alison, when you tell me I don't love you (Describe) it makes me feel both awful and misunderstood (Express), because I do love you very much. If you're feeling unloved, I wish you'd tell me right away and we can talk about it (Specify). Maybe then we can figure out what happens rather than getting into arguments about what I feel (Outcome)."

"I keep running out of money before the end of the month and I don't know how I'll get by (Describe). That makes me really anxious (Express). Would you be willing to sit down with me over coffee and go over my finances to see what I can do about this (Specify)? I'd really appreciate it (Outcome)."

Checkpoint: Writing a DESO Script

Choose a specific situation in your own life in which you would like to request a change or a favor of some kind. Come up with a DESO script to deal with it.

Who is involved? _____

Situation: _____

_____

Now write down the actual statements you could make for each stage.

Describe: _____

_____

_____

Express: _____

_____

_____

Specify: _____

_____

_____

Outcome: _____

_____

_____

Do you need extra paper? If so, your script is too long. Whether you needed extra room or not, review your script and trim it down to the basics. Try to make it clear *and* brief.

Practice Session: Making Requests Assertively

In this exercise your task is to rehearse making an assertive request using a DESO script. This is easiest if you work with a partner, though it can be done without.

Think of a situation in which you would like to make a request of someone. If you like, you can use the request from the previous exercise. Alternatively, pick a scenario from the list below.

- Ask a friend of yours to teach you how to ski.

- Request that a fellow airplane passenger trade seats with you.

- Your friend never uses her car on the weekend; ask if you can borrow it.

- Ask a fellow committee member to be the new treasurer.

- Ask a friend to drive you to and from your appointment to have your wisdom teeth removed.

- You want your spouse or partner to come with you when you visit your parents next week.

- You're moving this weekend; ask a friend to help you.

- Ask your boss to refrain from giving you new work while you get caught up.

- Ask your teenager to call you if he'll be home later than 10 PM.

- Request that the hotel manager move you to a room farther from the noisy pub.

- Ask the person doing your home repairs to give you a firm completion date.

- Request that your landlord give you notice before showing your apartment to potential new tenants.

Develop a DESO script. See if you can think it through in your head, though you should feel free to write it down if necessary.

If you are working alone, deliver your request to the mirror. Watch your nonverbal behavior and listen to your voice as you do so. Imagine what it would be like to receive this request. How would you respond? If you are imagining making the request of someone in your life, how do you think they would respond? What would you say then?

If you are working with someone else, brief your partner on the situation and the kind of person you are imagining them to be. For example: *"I'm asking this of my brother, who always tries to get out of any kind of responsibility."* Then deliver your script.

If you are the receiver, notice how it feels to hear this request. You should not go along with the request completely, at least at first. Respond as you think you really would in this situation—or as you think the person you are playing would (e.g., the brother). The asker then has the opportunity to respond to the receiver's reply; then the receiver can respond again.

Discuss how the exercise went. What was it like for the asker to make a request this way? How did the receiver feel hearing it? Did the asker give any sign of expecting to be turned down? Was there anything that could have been done better?

When you have finished the discussion, the asker should have the chance to reword the script and try again. Then switch roles. Repeat the exercise several times.

Practice Session: DESO Scripts in Action

For the coming week, come up with at least one situation in which you feel your needs, desires, or expectations are not being met. Think about the situation in advance and write out a DESO script for yourself beforehand. Rehearse the elements of your script. Then put it into action.

When you choose the situation, keep in mind that making requests may be an unfamiliar and difficult skill for you. You will need to pick a situation that is not too challenging. Think of the following scale:

Level One: Requesting a table reservation at a restaurant.
Asking someone to pass the butter at dinner.

Level Two: Returning a defective product to a department store.
Asking a neighbor to take in your newspaper while you are away.

Level Three: Assigning a new and ongoing chore to a member of the family.
Requesting that a neighbor pay for damage to your property.

Level Four: Expressing dissatisfaction with your partner's behavior.
Protesting unfair treatment from a work supervisor.

Consider how difficult you would find the situations described at each level. Are they easy, challenging, or impossible? You should start off with a situation that is *mildly* challenging. Maybe you are hoping to learn how to handle the Level Four type of situation. Even so, start out with something much easier.

What is the situation?

_____

_____

Now write out a DESO script for this situation in the space below. Trim it down to the essentials, just as you did in the last exercise.

Describe: _____

_____

_____

Express: _____

_____

_____

Specify: _____

_____

_____

Outcome: _____

_____

_____

Once you are satisfied with your script, reread it until you have it almost memorized. You won't have to recite the script word for word, but you should remember the basics. Make your request when the opportunity arises. Use an Assertiveness Scorecard to record how it went. What was the outcome? What did you do well? What could you have done better?

Consider repeating the exercise with other situations in your life.

CHAPTER 15

COUNTDOWN TO CONFRONTATION

You are a unique human being with a unique perspective. There is no one quite like you *anywhere on earth*. Think about what this means. It means that you will never have a relationship in which you and the other person agree on every issue. It means that in *every* close relationship you have for the rest of your life, there will be points of difference between you and the other person. Some of those differences will lead to conflict.

The title of this chapter may sound foreboding. To some people, the very word "confrontation" sounds negative, something to be suppressed. It isn't. The *Oxford English Dictionary* defines confrontation as "the bringing of persons face-to-face." In the lexicon of this book, confrontation is the act of bringing both parties onstage, to *be there* together. A confrontation occurs when two or more people attempt to cope with a conflict. It needn't be an unpleasant or acrimonious exchange to count as a confrontation.

Differences cannot be avoided. Confrontations can. You can pretend that you don't really differ. You can deny your likes, dislikes, preferences, values, and goals. *"Oh, no, I didn't mean that. I feel the same as you."* Or you can deny the *other* person's likes, dislikes, preferences, values, and goals. *"You don't know what you want. I know what you want."* But avoidance doesn't solve the problem, and neither does self-centeredness. To solve the problem—to *be there*—you have to deal with the conflict. You must be willing to confront the issue.

Here are some examples of common confrontations:

- Deciding who will carry out family responsibilities.

- Setting boundaries with children.

- Dealing with a coworker who interferes with your work.

- Deciding on spending priorities with your spouse.

- Dividing up chores between housemates.

- Discussing work assignments with supervisors.

Confrontations can be profoundly difficult. They often go wrong. People become anxious, feel threatened, become angry. They yell, wave their arms, and exaggerate. The exchange often makes things worse rather than better.

Why are these situations so challenging? There are several reasons.

- **Complexity.** Unlike many situations, confrontations require almost all of the skills involved in assertive communication: using body language effectively, giving your opinion, offering feedback, receiving feedback, refusing unreasonable requests, and making requests of your own. A breakdown in any of these skills can send the exchange off the rails.

- **Importance of the relationship.** Conflicts often arise in crucial relationships: boss, employee, spouse, best friend, child. The more important the relationship and the more history you have with the person, the more threatening a conflict can be. What if your partner leaves you? What if your child overdoses on drugs? What if your boss thinks you are unreliable? What if your child's obstinacy is a sign of difficult teenage years to come? What if the job never changes and you're stuck like this until retirement? Such fears can make it easy to become upset and get off track during a confrontation.

- **Importance of the issue.** Conflict often arises over issues of great importance to us: the fidelity of a spouse, responsibilities at work, the safety of a child. We may be willing to give way on less important matters (who buys the toothpaste, who answers the phone most often, who gets up earlier), but when the issue seems crucial we often feel compelled to take a rigid, uncompromising stand. If the other person does the same, a power struggle usually ensues.

- **Symbolic value.** Some situations have great symbolic value to us. Conflicts over the cap on the toothpaste tube, the position of the toilet seat, and flowers on the anniversary have little to do with toothpaste, toilets, or flowers. They concern the symbolism of the other person's behavior. Leaving the cap off the toothpaste means you think I'm your servant. Leaving the seat up means you don't care about women. No flowers means the love is gone and the marriage is headed for the rocks. The conflict is often played out around the issue at hand (toothpaste), not the *real* issue (*"Do you love me?"*). It's hard to resolve a conflict when the real issue isn't ever discussed.

- **Length.** Confrontations often require considerable discussion, clarification, and decision-making. It can be hard to prepare ahead of time, because the other person will often respond unpredictably. You need to be able to think on your feet and to maintain an assertive stance for a longer time than with many other situations.

Checkpoint: Preparing for Confrontation

It helps to prepare yourself for confrontations before they begin. This isn't always possible. Some conflicts happen unexpectedly. You find yourself in a confrontation before you know what's happening, and for some reason you can't put it off. Fortunately, this usually isn't the case.

This chapter provides a set of suggestions to assist you in preparing for confrontation. It will be helpful for you to have a specific conflict situation in mind as you go over the ideas presented. Pick a conflict from your own life that you would like to deal with. Take a moment and briefly describe the situation.

Who does your conflict involve? _____

What is the issue? _____

_____

_____

_____

Perhaps you can decide when to raise this issue with the person involved. Alternatively, perhaps you know that the confrontation will happen sooner or later—but you're not sure exactly when. Or perhaps if the issue comes up unexpectedly, you will be able to put it off until you have had time to think. All of these situations allow you a chance to prepare.

Here is a sequence of ten steps designed to help you plan ahead.

Step One: State the Issue to Yourself

What is the problem, exactly? Initially the problem may be a vague impression that something is not quite right. *"I feel like I am being taken advantage of."* This points us to a general principle about confrontations:

Key point: You cannot solve an impression; you can only solve a problem.

In other words, your impression is based on something—maybe a belief, maybe someone's behavior, maybe something someone told you, maybe, as Scrooge thought, nothing more than "a bit of undigested beef." There's nothing wrong with having an impression. Indeed, becoming aware of your impressions may be essential before you can do anything else. But in order to take action you need to go further.

What's bugging you? You don't have to come up with a solution just yet, but you *do* have to know what the problem is.

You've identified one problem above. Take a look and see if the issue is relatively clear. If not, perhaps you have defined your *impression* as the problem. *"I'm feeling used." "I'm resentful at work." "I'm wishing I'd never become a parent."* See if you can figure out what the impression is based on. *"My relationship with my daughter is unfulfilling because she ignores my requests and shows no interest in being around me."* Better.

If necessary, reword your identified problem to focus on the issue, not your reaction to it.

_____

_____

_____

Perhaps you don't know what the real issue is. Perhaps at work or in your marriage you have a general sense of malaise that seems almost undefinable. If so, try doing some brainstorming. Sit down with pen and paper and try to come up with every possible factor that might contribute even the tiniest amount to your impression. The search for the single cause of your dissatisfaction is usually a misplaced quest. Chances are, there is no single factor. Most problems are caused by multiple factors.

Once you have identified the contributing factors, you may want to deal with all of them. More often, though, you will find it better to choose one aspect of the problem for attention, rather than the whole thing.

Step Two: Find the Symbolic Value

Is the conflict really about the issue you have defined, or is it about what the issue *means* about you and the relationship? What does the conflict or difficulty symbolize to you?

Consider an example: You have a coworker who frequently takes office supplies from your desk. There might be a number of reasons why this would lead to conflict. One would be that your own work gets slowed down when you have to go looking for things. Another might be that you could get into trouble for using more supplies than you have been allotted. A third might be that you interpret what this behavior means about the relationship between the coworker and yourself:

"She thinks that because she's been here longer, I should be her servant."

"He's doing this because he's a racist."

"She's an inconsiderate slob."

"He's been told by the boss to go through my desk as part of a company-wide plot to check up on me."

Your reaction, including your distress, may be due more to what you think the situation symbolizes than to what is really going on. *"He doesn't love me"* rather than *"He leaves the seat up." "I'm about to be fired"* rather than *"She pointed out an error in my work." "I've raised a delinquent child"* rather than *"She drew pictures on the wall."*

Why do events have such strong symbolic value for us? Sometimes we draw valid conclusions from others' behavior. Most of the time, though, our symbolic value has as much to do with our own minds and our own history as it does with the situation at hand. A previous partner cheated on us, so we get suspicious every time the current one comes home late. We feel inadequate, so every time the boss frowns we imagine we're about to be fired. We feel unlovable, so every sign of independence on the part of our children means we are inadequate parents.

It's vital to know what the symbolic value of a conflict is for us. That way we can evaluate it and consider whether:

1. to base the confrontation on the symbolic value (*"I need to ask whether he's having an affair"*);

2. to base the confrontation on the actual behavior (*"I want him to help keep the bathroom clean"*); or

3. to discard the confrontation because the real problem is our own perception (*"Maybe his reading in the bathtub doesn't mean he's rejecting me"*).

Consider the situation you have identified. What does it *mean* to you that this is happening or has happened? What are you afraid it *might* mean?

_____

_____

_____

Which do you want to deal with more: the actual situation, or what you think it means? Which seems more appropriate, given the nature of the situation?

_____

Dealing with the actual situation is considerably easier in most cases. If you choose to work on the symbolic value, then your first step is to ask yourself how certain you are that your interpretation is correct. What is the evidence? If you are satisfied that your interpretation is plausible, then you may wish to discuss the matter with the person (after working through the other steps in this section). The best stance for this is usually an invitation to discussion rather than confronting the person with your pre-established assumptions. So rather than, *"OK, John, what did I do wrong?"* you could say, *"John, I'm concerned that you're not returning my calls because I have offended you in some way. Could that be true?"*

Step Three: Describe the Problem in Behavioral Terms

What is the problem, exactly? Initially the problem may be a general impression that something is not right. *"My son is too inconsiderate."* If you tell your son that you think he is too inconsiderate, what will happen? He will feel insulted and he will defend himself by attempting to prove you wrong. *"What are you talking about? Last March I pruned the rose bushes!"* This type of confrontation will lead nowhere.

So what can you do? Before you begin the confrontation, define the problem as clearly as possible. Be specific about what you would like to be different. Focus on behavior rather than personality as much as possible. What are you or the other person doing that you don't like?

"What am I really upset about? Well . . . in March we agreed that he would mow the lawn every week and he's only done it every three weeks, with a lot of nagging from me. He leaves his coat and shoes on the floor in the front hall. He eats in his room and leaves the dishes there until the food rots. He uses the car and, as far as I can tell, has never filled it with gas."

Don't wait to define the problem until you are in the middle of the confrontation. At that point, you will be distracted by the other person and you may be anxious or angry. These factors will make it more difficult to think clearly. The more unclear you are about the problem, the less likely it is that the confrontation will go well.

Sometimes the process of defining the problem will lead to some realizations on your part. You may see the situation from the other person's perspective. You might discover reasons for their behavior that you hadn't previously considered. You may be able to let go of the hidden belief that the other person is really a villain. *"What's really bothering me is that he agreed to care for the rose bushes this year and all he did was prune them in March. Maybe he thinks that's all you need to do. I never told him about fertilizing or any of the other tasks. Maybe the problem is not that he's inconsiderate. Maybe it's that we didn't communicate well enough before he took on the job."*

Go back to the conflict that you have selected. Rewrite it as a set of very specific, observable behaviors or events. Eliminate your guesses about the motivation of the other person (*"He secretly likes it when I'm angry"*), even if you think you're right. If you still see the problem as a personality trait of the other person (*"She's unreliable"*), write down the specific events or behaviors that make you think this way.

_____

_____

_____

_____

Step Four: Define Your Goal

What do you *want*? Perhaps you are just angry and want to let it out, jump up and down, and scream. Unfortunately, this usually leads to the other person responding in the same way. As a result, simply venting anger is usually unsatisfying. Generally it is better to think of exactly how you want things to change.

Remember not to state your goal in terms of personality change. *"I would like her to be more reliable." "I want to be able to trust him." "She should be smarter about her work."* None of us can change our personalities at will. If anything changes, it will be behavior.

It may be difficult to decide what you want. You may not know. Perhaps the reason for the conflict is your feeling of anger, or frustration, or distrust, or boredom. It can be valuable to share these feelings with the other person. But if you are asking for change, you will have to be specific. Asking the other person to *"be smarter"* will only lead to more frustration for you both. Here are some examples of specific goals:

- *"I would like my son to mow the lawn once a week without prompting."*

- *"I would like my helper to save up her questions about the job and ask them only twice a day rather than phoning me every few minutes."*

- *"I would like him to call me if he's going to be home more than two hours late."*

- *"I would like her to tell me that she's tired when we're skiing rather than trying to keep up with me."*

We often have a *secret goal*. We secretly want others to admit that they are villains, that they *intended* to hurt or frustrate us, and that we ourselves are completely innocent of any wrongdoing. Sometimes this is appropriate. We really do want them to take responsibility for their own behavior. It can be appropriate to express this desire. *"I would like you to stop blaming me for your affair and to take responsibility for your own actions."*

In many situations, however, our own anger makes us fantasize about total victory over the other person. *"You're right, I should never have asked you to work late (sniffle); I'm the worst manager in the company!"* Here the task is to recognize that we have this perfectly normal thirst for victory—and then to let it go. Face facts. You probably won't get this admission of total guilt. Even if you do get it, it won't be as satisfying as you might think. Some people admit guilt (*"You're right, I'm just evil . . . "*) as a way of avoiding responsibility for their future actions (*". . . so I can't change"*). *"Honey, alcoholism is a disease, so I can't be held responsible for any of my actions."* In general, it's best to focus on behavior rather than on convincing people they are wrong.

What is your goal in the conflict situation you have chosen? Is there more than one goal?

_____

_____

_____

Step Five: Is It Really You Who Needs to Change?

Sometimes when you define the problem and the goal, you realize that you're upset about something *you* are doing. *"We're always going to the beach, and I hate the beach—though, come to think of it, I never say so." "He's always asking for favors and I'm constantly doing things for him and getting nothing in return."* The temptation can be to attack the other person and want them to change. *"You're so inconsiderate, constantly dragging me off to the beach! Stop asking me to go." "You're so dependent! Don't ask for so much of my time!"*

Instead, perhaps *you* need to change. If you don't like going to the beach, perhaps *you* need to say so and then not go. If you want to cut back on the unappreciated favors, perhaps *you* need to say no more often. Sometimes this can eliminate the need for a confrontation altogether. Instead, you may just want to let the other person know about the change. *"I noticed recently that I was doing so much of your work that mine was slipping—so I'm going to be less available in future."*

In your chosen conflict situation, how do *you* need to change?

_____

_____

_____

Step Six: Pick Your Battles

You don't have to be assertive all the time. Assertiveness is always about choice. *Your* choice. Sometimes you may choose to let the issue pass without being assertive.

How important is the situation? Maybe it doesn't really matter what happens. If your aunt gives you tea that you don't want, you might just drink it anyway or set it aside. If Frank the architect wants you to see his favorite building, you might go along with him even if you're not really interested. It doesn't matter. Sometimes it's more interesting to allow yourself to go along with others' plans or wishes. You have the option of assertively stating your preferences and declining unwanted requests. You need not always act on this option.

Some minor issues can act as "hooks" for your own emotions. Unimportant matters can drive you crazy, if you let them. Perhaps your spouse constantly wears mismatched clothes or leaves the garage door open. You can make it a big issue if you like, but why bother? You probably won't change the other person, and focusing on the issue may only stir up resentment between the two of you. The task in many of these situations is 1) to communicate your preferences but then 2) to *let go* of the attempt to change the person. Let them wear the wrong colors, leave the door open, squeeze the toothpaste in the middle, or drop towels on the floor. Let them know what you would like, but then choose *not* to make it an ongoing conflict.

A related point is that in general you should only fight battles you can win. Life is short. You only have so much energy. Why waste it unless the effort will get you somewhere? If you have been trying for thirty years to get your mother to stop asking when you will get married, give up. Let her ask. If you have been trying for years to get your partner to be faithful, perhaps it's time to stop trying—and either accept the behavior or end the relationship. If asking your daughter to quit smoking never works and only gets you both upset, give up. She'll quit when she decides to quit. Your badgering may be preventing her from finding her own reasons for quitting.

The battles that you can't win have something in common. You are usually trying to control the behavior of the other person. Remember the core principle of assertiveness: **Assertiveness is about controlling your behavior, not anyone else's.** If you catch yourself saying, *"I've tried and tried to be assertive and nothing works,"* sit back and think about it. Just who are you trying to control?

Take a look at your chosen conflict situation. Is this issue important to you? Is it really a problem, or is it just a "hook" for your mind to obsess about? Is change really possible? (Some of these answers only become clear once you have done the rest of your preparation. Be willing to come back and look at this issue again.)

Step Seven: Write a DESO Script

DESO scripts are discussed in detail in chapter 14. Such scripts are also useful in preparing for confrontations. Briefly, write out one or two sentences on each of four topics: **Describe** exactly what you find unsatisfying. **Express** how you feel about the situation. **Specify** what you would like to happen (your goals). State the **Outcome** you foresee if things do or do not work out the way you would like.

For example:

Describe: *I notice that the lawn hasn't been cut in some time. I remember that a couple of months ago we agreed that it would be your job to cut it once a week.*

Express: *I don't like to see it get that long, but I feel frustrated nagging you about it all the time.*

Specify: *I'd like it to be done once a week, as we agreed earlier.*

Outcome: *That way I won't feel I have to get after you about it.* (And possibly: *Then you can watch television that week.* Or: *And you can borrow my car on Mondays and Thursdays.*)

Now put it all together. Come up with a DESO script for your chosen conflict situation.

Describe: _____

_____

_____

Express: _____

_____

_____

Specify: _____

_____

_____

Outcome: _____

_____

_____

Step Eight: Choose Your Place

Where do you want to have the discussion? Some people like to choose public places (such as restaurants) for certain issues because the other person is more reasonable in those settings. At other times you may want a more private setting. If there is a potential for violence (for example, if you have an abusive mate), be sure to include this in your considerations regarding setting.

Remember, though: No one likes to be embarrassed in public. Whenever you confront someone, strive to ensure that the situation is as private as possible. Avoid confronting others in front of their friends, family, or colleagues. If you choose a restaurant, ensure that you will be able to have your discussion privately. If you choose to have a mediator present, try to select someone who will be acceptable to both of you.

Where would be the best place to have your confrontation?

_____

_____

Step Nine: Choose Your Time

Don't start a confrontation five minutes before you have to leave for a dental appointment. Pick a time when both you and the other person are available and have enough time to deal with the issue. This should be a time when you are reasonably calm and focused. If you are usually tired or irritable late in the afternoon, pick another time.

Sometimes choosing your time means deciding when you will raise the issue. Sometimes it means negotiating with the other person about a time to talk. Regardless, choosing a time means you may have to initiate the discussion yourself. This may be difficult for you if you are used to a more passive approach. Instead of avoiding confrontation, you will be actively pursuing it.

What if the other person springs the confrontation on you? Remember that you have the right to control your own behavior. This includes taking part in discussions about difficult issues. You have control over when you will and will not be willing to talk—or even *whether* you are willing to discuss an issue at all. If the issue comes up when you are not ready to discuss it, feel free to ask for time to think about it.

- *"I have to leave for my appointment in just a few minutes. When would be a good time for us to set aside to talk about this?"*

- *"I need some time to think out what I want to say. Would you be willing to meet Thursday evening to talk about it?"*

When would be a good time for you and the other person to discuss the issue?

Have you had to put off this confrontation at some point? If the issue comes up when you're not ready to deal with it, what could you say?

Step Ten: Ensure Your Safety

If you are thinking about confronting someone who may become violent (such as an abusive spouse), ensure that you have adequately protected yourself first. Perhaps there are other issues that need to be resolved before you tackle this situation. If you do need to confront the person, are you safe?

Perhaps it would be a good idea to have someone else present. Perhaps you should have your discussion with the aid of a professional, such as a counselor or professional mediator. Perhaps you should pick a setting where others would be available in the event of trouble or where the person you confront would not become violent. *Never*, however, use a child as a mediator or witness in a difficult confrontation between spouses—even if doing so would eliminate the potential for violence.

This brief discussion is not sufficient to go over all of the factors involved in dealing with conflict in violent relationships. If you have a relationship such as this, you may be best advised to get extra help or counseling in dealing with it.

Is there a risk of violence in the situation you have selected?

If so, what steps will you take to ensure your safety?

_____

_____

_____

There you have it. Ten steps. When you get to the end, you may notice that you still haven't started dealing with the issue. But maybe you're more prepared. Put a hand on your stomach, breathe deeply, and read the next chapter.

CHAPTER 16

CONSTRUCTIVE CONFRONTATION

So you've identified an issue. You've thought about it, you've realized that you really do need to work it out with the person involved, and you've worked your way through the steps identified in the last chapter. You have your plan and you know what you want to say. It's time to get to work.

Sooner or later the confrontation begins. Hopefully you are in a safe, comfortable environment where you can communicate both clearly and openly. The following is a set of recommendations to consider as the exchange occurs. You'll want to read them now, though, to help you be ready.

You have already worked to identify which of the styles of communication you use most often and which nonassertive style is the most tempting for you. This will be important to bear in mind as you consider the recommendations. If you often behave aggressively, the risk of confrontation is that you will slide into aggression if the exchange becomes difficult. Pay special attention to those suggestions that will help you to deal with competitive or hostile impulses. If the passive style is most attractive to you, the temptation will be to avoid the confrontation altogether or to give in to the other person's view at the first sign of disagreement. As you read the chapter, watch for strategies that will help you hold your position. If passive-aggressive behavior has been a habit, the pull in confrontations is to become indirect or sarcastic. Strategies that will help you to retain a candid, direct style will be the most critical to remember.

Relax

Confrontations make most people a little nervous. You may fear that the exchange will go badly. Or the issue involved may make you angry or frustrated. These emotions help to activate the stress response. The stress response, in turn, inhibits assertive responding, pulling you more and more toward a passive or aggressive stance. The more you adopt a nonassertive stance, the more likely it is that the exchange will falter. If you become passive, you will be unable to get your point across effectively. If you are aggressive, the other person will usually avoid the issue or become aggressive in return. The more the exchange veers away from a productive discussion, the more you feel fearful or frustrated. As a result, the stress response gets activated even more. Here it is in graphic form:

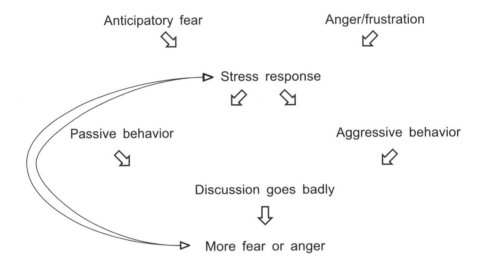

In other words, we have here a classic vicious circle that is likely to spiral out of control.

Where can you intervene to stop the spiral? One spot is at the stress response. If you reduce the tension, you reduce the likelihood of engaging in passive or aggressive behavior. How do you do that? Relaxation. Take some time to calm yourself just before you confront someone. Perform a thorough relaxation exercise if you know one. Alternatively, take time out for a few minutes of diaphragmatic breathing or meditation. You will be much more effective at communicating if you can remain reasonably relaxed.

It is also important to relax *during* the discussion. You may find yourself holding your breath or breathing shallowly and rapidly without using your diaphragm. Remind yourself to breathe. Concentrate on slowing the pace of your breathing and increasing the volume of air you take in with each breath. You may find it helpful to place a hand casually over your stomach so that you can monitor your breathing as the confrontation takes place. The other person probably won't notice what you are doing. Even if they do, nothing is lost.

What could you do to help you to remain calm and relaxed in the situation you identified in chapter 15?

_____

_____

Watch Your Body Language

During confrontations it is easy to become very tense. You may clench your fists, hunch your shoulders, wrinkle your brow, and grit your teeth. Perhaps you will adopt an aggressive posture (move in too close, stare the other person down, wear an angry expression). This stance is likely to put others on the defensive or may cause them to become aggressive in return.

Alternatively, you may adopt a passive posture due to fear (looking down, angling your body toward the floor, seldom making eye contact, wearing a fearful expression, clutching your hands together). This will make it look like you don't really believe in your position.

Instead, adopt an open and relaxed posture. Sit back, keep a moderate amount of eye contact, let go of facial tension, smile when appropriate, avoid fidgeting, and angle your body gently toward the other person. This stance communicates an expectation that the conflict can be resolved and that you will neither attack nor be attacked. It can be difficult to maintain this posture when inside you are feeling angry or frightened. Nevertheless, it can be very helpful to hold as relaxed a posture as you can, even if this means faking it a bit. The posture itself can affect your mind, helping you to calm yourself and stay present in the discussion.

Which aspect of your nonverbal behavior will you have to concentrate on the most?

_____

_____

Maintain an Even Voice

As with your posture, maintain a vocal tone that communicates assertiveness rather than aggression or passivity. An even, clear, well-modulated, and friendly tone can do much to defuse the potential anger in a confrontation. Don't get too loud. Don't start to whisper. If the other person begins talking too loudly or too softly, do your best not to follow their lead. Instead, keep your voice at a normal volume and a friendly tone. If the other person becomes aggressively loud, deliberately lowering and calming your own voice may help to relax the situation.

How does your voice typically change during confrontations?

_____

_____

Listen for this change during your confrontation and concentrate on returning it to an even, calm tone.

Start with Bonding

Most people feel threatened by conflict, and feeling threatened makes us react badly. When we are confronted we wonder whether the friendship or relationship is over or whether we are about to be fired. Before you begin talking about your differences, it can be helpful to cement the relationship. Talk about what you *do* like before saying what you *don't* like. This can calm the person and help them to see that you are talking about a specific problem, not about their total worth as a human being.

- *"First off, let me say that I've been pleased with your work overall the last few months. . . ."*

- *"I'm really enjoying travelling with you. . . ."*

- *"Look at all the work you've finished, Katie. Well done!"*

Statements such as these place a boundary around the problem you want to discuss. You show people that they are valued and respected. They do not have to worry that you will reject them entirely or that the conflict arises from your hatred of them. A warning, however: In all relationships, remember to give positive messages such as these at other times as well, without following up with a confrontation. Otherwise people will rightly view your compliments with suspicion. *"Oh great, a compliment. Here comes the bad stuff."*

In the confrontation you have identified, could you start with something positive? How?

_____

_____

_____

Use Your DESO Script

Remember the four parts of your script. Be as clear and concise as you can. Focus on the positive as much as possible (*"I'd like to enjoy my time with you more than I do . . ."*) and get to the point.

Don't overelaborate. You will find it tempting to go on at length about your point. The person will stop hearing you quite quickly. They may be looking at you, but they're thinking about what they're going to say in return. The longer you speak, the more you frustrate them by holding them back from responding. The more frustrated they become, the less likely they are to respond without aggression.

You may worry that the person won't understand you if you don't go on at length. If the person doesn't understand you, they can ask for clarification and you can give it. The confrontation is an exchange, not a monologue.

There is also a hidden motivation behind the tendency to go on at length. It is a fear of what the other person will say in response. The natural tendency associated with fear is avoidance. The way to avoid hearing the response is to prevent it from taking place by continuing to talk. Instead, face your fear. State your point, then sit back and allow the response to come.

It can also be a good idea to hold back any negative consequences in your outcome statement unless it is a longstanding issue. Giving the negative consequences early (*". . . otherwise I'll talk to your employer . . ."*) can come across as a threat. This may cause the person to become more resistant to your message than they would be otherwise. *"I'm not going to cave in to threats!"* Instead, it can be best to give the positive outcome you hope for in the initial DESO script. *". . . and then I think we'll get along much better."* This provides the other person the option of responding positively without the threatened negative consequence on the table. If they do not respond well, you can raise the negative consequence later in the exchange. *"Hank, I've decided that if this doesn't change, I will leave you."* If you have had the confrontation repeatedly and nothing has helped, then you might wish to present the negative consequence earlier.

With children you may wish to make negative consequences a bit clearer than you might with adults, and you might give them somewhat earlier in the process. *". . . by eight p.m., or you won't be able to go on the sleepover."* It is often possible, however, to frame consequences positively. Rather than saying: *"No movie unless the garbage is out,"* you could say, *"And once the garbage is out you can watch the movie."* The latter statement presumes that your son will take the garbage out, whereas the former presumes that he won't. This principle applies to communication with adults as well but can be especially helpful with children.

If there are negative consequences in your DESO script, how could you frame them positively? Is it appropriate to do so?

Take Responsibility

Use "I" messages to tell the other person how the situation affects you and what you want. Take responsibility for your actions and your requests. Avoid saying things like, *"Every other family does it this way."* Appealing to outside authority (everyone else, your psychologist, your brother's family, this book) denies your personal responsibility for your opinion and invites an argument. *"Prove to me that everyone does that." "That's not a fair example." "I don't go along with everything your stupid assertiveness book says."*

In a similar vein, avoid blaming your emotions on the other person's behavior. *"You make me feel miserable when you do that."* It may seem true, but your emotions are *your* responsibility, not theirs. Trying to make others responsible for how you feel will put them on the defensive. Few problems are solved this way. Here's a better way of putting it: *"When that happens I feel miserable."* The difference is subtle, but important.

Also take responsibility for your choice of consequences and your decision to act on them. *"If this doesn't change, I plan to begin searching for another position."* Avoid blaming the consequences on the other person with "you" statements. *"You leave me no choice." "You will force me to take legal action."* These statements are not really true. The person isn't forcing you to do anything. You are *choosing* to react in a certain way. Admit it. Make it clear that your response will depend on theirs (*"... if you don't do it, then I will ..."*), but don't deny that it is still your choice.

When you are in a confrontation do you find yourself avoiding responsibility by appealing to authority? By blaming your emotions on the other person? By blaming your actions on the other person?

_____

_____

How might this occur in the conflict you have been thinking about? What would you like to do instead?

_____

_____

_____

Don't Try To Win

When we get into confrontations we often have a hidden fantasy about the outcome. We'd like the other person to take complete responsibility for the problem and then to change in accordance with our desires, relieving us of the necessity of examining our own beliefs or behavior. We want total victory.

This seldom happens. Few confrontations are resolved by having one person give in completely and grant total victory to the other. Instead, effective confrontation usually involves mutual problem solving and compromise. Here are some examples:

- *"So you're saying that you think the grass only needs cutting every ten days, not every week. I'd be willing to agree to that, but only if it means it really gets done without my nagging you."*

- *"Tell you what: I like going to the beach a couple of times a year, but not every weekend. How about the whole family going once a month during the summer, and you go without me the rest of the time, taking the kids when they want to go."*

To reach this kind of resolution, you have to be aware of your fantasy outcome, including your desire for total victory. You should treat these desires of yours with some compassion. It is perfectly understandable that you want to win. But in most situations, you must let go of the unrealistic elements of those desires and open your mind to the possibility of another solution. Doing so will enable you to hear what the other person has to say.

What would be a fantasy outcome in the situation you have identified? What would you really like to happen? Be honest. No one has to see this book.

_____

_____

_____

What could you tell yourself that might help you to let go of this fantasy outcome, at least until you have really heard what the other person has to say?

_____

_____

_____

Avoid Old History

In the heat of the moment it can be tempting to bring up other issues— including unresolved problems from the distant past. *"And do you remember the time you. . . ."* Conflict over one topic is hard enough to handle. Don't bring up others. When we bring up old history, it is almost always because we have been seduced by our own anger. We are trying either to win or to hurt the other person. Both are understandable impulses, but both make the conflict worse. Stay on topic.

What old history will you feel tempted to bring up? How will you keep yourself on topic?

_____

_____

_____

Absolutely No Absolutes

The more convinced we are of our position, the more tempting it is to use absolutes:

- *"You never do the dishes!"*
- *"You're always late!"*
- *"You constantly give me new work before I've even taken my coat off."*
- *"Every time I come in here the same thing happens."*

- *"Whenever I see you you're taking a personal call."*

- *"You invariably get drunk on Fridays."*

There are others: everything, nothing, all the time, none of the time, and so on. The common feature is that they all say, *"My statement is true in every case."* In almost every case, however, the statement is a lie. It isn't true that the same thing happens *every* day. It isn't true that the other person is *always* late. We're exaggerating.

What's the big deal? These words still convey the main point, don't they?

Well, no. Absolute statements usually derail constructive discussion. The other person will find it unbearably tempting to prove you wrong. *"Hah! I did the dishes once in August!"* and they will usually be right. You lose, and your point (wanting them to help out more often) has been lost.

What you usually mean is that something happens *more often* or *less often* than you would like. *"You do the dishes sometimes, but usually I do them."* If this is what you mean, *say so*. The other person won't feel as tempted to argue, and it will be easier to stay on topic. Don't get pulled into absolutes unless you really mean them.

Think of an absolute statement you could make about your issue.

Imagine that someone is telling *you* this. Can you feel the temptation to argue the point? Even if you can't think of an exception to the statement you want to make, rest assured that the other person will. Reword it as a more accurate statement, replacing absolute words with relative ones, such as: "more often," "less often," "frequently," "infrequently," and so on. Word it so that it sounds natural for you to say.

Although this statement may sound weaker to you, it probably has more strength because it has more truth in it.

Listen

During confrontations we are often so wrapped up in our own opinion and what we want to say next that we don't listen. The other person usually senses this, becomes frustrated, and stops listening as well. No conflict can be solved without communication, and no communication can occur without listening.

Pay attention to the points the other person makes. Show that you are listening. When you think you understand what they are saying, say it back to them in your own words. This is called a *reflection of content*. Don't twist it. *"So you're saying I'm stupid, is that it?"* This only shows that you *weren't* listening. If the other person doesn't agree that you have it right, *then you don't.* To resolve the conflict you have to understand their viewpoint. You don't have to agree with it, but you do have to understand it. If you don't understand it, you can't solve the problem. *"OK, let me see if I'm understanding you. When I ask you to be on time, you feel a bit like you're trapped, as though your life is not your own anymore. Like you're a little kid having to be on time for school. Is that close?"*

Show that you see how the other person feels. Make a simple statement about the feelings that the person seems to be experiencing. This is called a *reflection of emotion* and typically helps the other person to feel that they have been heard. Acknowledge those feelings, and do not insult the person for having them. *"You're really frustrated by this. I never realized how important it is to you."*

If you have discussed your issue with this person before, how much have you been able to listen? (Yes, yes, we all know *they* don't listen. But do *you*? Really?)

As you have been thinking about this issue, you have probably been imagining how the other person will react. Take one of these imagined reactions and come up with a reflection of content.

Now try a reflection of emotion.

Are either of these any good? Test them out. Put yourself in the other person's shoes. Imagine that you are on the opposite side of the issue, hearing the reflections you have written. How would you react?

To the reflection of content: _____

To the reflection of emotion: _____

If you would react badly to either, rephrase the reflection and try again. This is no guarantee that the other person will react the same way, but it's a reasonable method of taking the hidden barbs out of your statements.

Find Common Ground

What are you doing in the confrontation? Hopefully you are clarifying an issue. You are identifying the specific points on which you agree and other points on which you disagree. When you start out, it may seem as though you disagree completely. For example, if you are talking about buying a new home, perhaps you think your partner's priorities are completely wrong-headed and they think the same of yours. How are you ever going to come up with a mutual decision?

As you talk, you will find that there are certain points you agree on. Good. You will need this common ground to build a new understanding. If you only focus on the points of disagreement, it will seem as though you have completely different ideas when really you don't. Perhaps you both think that the children need their own bedrooms and neither of you cares whether you have a fireplace. Find the common ground. Point it out and check it out. *"It sounds like we don't disagree completely. We both want a house rather than an apartment. We want enough bedrooms for each of the children. We want a backyard they can play in."*

Don't use this as a way of denying that the two of you disagree about some things, however. *"So there's really no problem, right?"* Clarify the points of disagreement as well. *"But it sounds like you'd like to live closer to work, whereas I want to be closer to the park. And you'd be willing to have a higher mortgage than I'm comfortable with. Is that right?"*

As you find more common ground, point it out. The differences are usually obvious, but as you talk you may find that they get smaller.

Do you already have any common ground with the other person on your issue? It may seem like the answer is no. If so, keep thinking. There usually is some. What is it?

_____

_____

_____

At the beginning of a confrontation the areas of disagreement or dispute usually seem massive and unmanageable, but they are usually somewhat vague as well. Are there things you'd like to clarify with the other person? What?

_____

_____

_____

One of the most important areas to understand is motivation. At the outset, you may find yourself thinking the person's motives are incomprehensible. *"No reasonable person could think behavior like that is appropriate."* If so, you probably don't understand their motives well enough. Often (though not always) the underlying motive is quite reasonable. *"If I live closer to work I'll be less exhausted at the end of the day, and I'm willing to pay to avoid commuting so far."* Sometimes you realize that you have the same motives and disagree only on the means to achieve them. *"We both want to have a good relationship. I think that having some separate interests helps the relationship by making it less constricting, whereas you feel that being together most of the time helps more."*

Do you think you and the other person share any motives when it comes to the issue you've been thinking about? What are they? Which motives would you like to understand more clearly as a result of your discussion?

_____

_____

_____

Give Points to the Other Side

During confrontations you may feel reluctant to acknowledge the good points made by the other person. This reluctance usually comes from a feeling of weakness or powerlessness. When we *already* feel the other person has the upper hand, we are reluctant to make them feel even stronger. When they make a good point, when they show that we were mistaken about something, when they respond well to something we have said, and when they point out the good things they have done, we are hesitant to agree with them. But if we don't give them credit for these points, they will feel we aren't listening to what they have to say. And they will be right.

What are we hoping for? We hope that they will listen to our side and acknowledge the truth in what we have to say. They will usually not do this unless we are willing to do the same for them. We may feel we are weakening our own position by agreeing with them. We aren't. If we build common ground and show that we are willing to listen, the other person will usually become more willing to listen to us.

In most conflicts, then, it is a good policy to give points to the other person. *"You're right, I'd forgotten that you worked on the garage while I did the spring cleaning." "I agree, you are considerate about most things." "Thank you for listening while I told my side of the problem."*

During past confrontations, how difficult has it been to acknowledge the good points made by the other person involved in your issue?

_____

_____

Can you think of a good point this person might make during a confrontation? What is it?

_____

_____

Imagine that they have made this point. What could you say to acknowledge it?

_____

_____

Don't Counterattack

When you confront people they will frequently become resentful or angry and lash out with accusations, insults, or counterattacks. You may think of these comments as "hooks": They can grab your emotions, catch your mind, and pull you away from the issue. They can be quite hurtful, and it is tempting to defend yourself against them.

Sometimes others know that they are trying to hook you. They "know your buttons" and deliberately push them to make you upset and to distract you. *"If you hadn't dropped out of school* (a big button for you), *you'd know that I'm right!" "Just because you have such a big nose* (a self-consciousness button), *you think you can sniff out the truth!"*

More often the other person doesn't know that they are hooking you or pushing your buttons. Couples often find that they cannot talk about certain issues without falling into hurtful arguments. Neither person has a clue how this happens. It just does. In reality, each says things that hook the other person's emotions, and the argument builds up from there.

The goal is *not* to prevent the other person from pushing your buttons or hooking you. You can't control their behavior. Instead, your goal should be to allow your buttons to be pushed and not to react. Don't respond to the hooks. If they bring up the size of your feet, let them. Don't comment. Just stay on topic. If they mention your obnoxious relatives, don't move in to defend your family. Stay on topic.

- Hook: *"You're not exactly faultless either, you know. Remember last spring when . . ."*

- Response: *"Right now we're talking about the lawn and I'd like us to stay with that. How often do you think . . ."*

- Hook: *"You're pretty pushy all of a sudden."*

- Response: *"Perhaps, but I'd really like to resolve this issue about our expenses."*

- Hook: *"This wouldn't be a problem if you'd sleep with me more often."*

- Response: *"Well, let's talk about that sometime. But right now I still want to decide who will pay the car insurance."*

With the issue you have been considering, how could the other person "hook" you away from the topic? Think of the strategies they have used in the past or areas where you know you are vulnerable.

_____

_____

_____

How could you respond to keep the discussion on topic?

_____

_____

_____

Keep Your Anger on a Leash

Many people feel that it is important to express every emotion. Indeed, self-expression can be helpful, especially when compared to emotional denial. In confrontation situations, however, aggression produces aggression. Communicating your anger by yelling, accusing the other person, or otherwise behaving aggressively is likely to produce an angry, aggressive response. The usual result is a back-and-forth escalation of anger—what some therapists think of as a *missile exchange*. He throws an insult, she throws a rock, he throws a grenade, she throws a bomb, he throws a missile, she throws a nuclear missile. Nothing gets resolved and the situation only gets worse.

If you *really* want to solve the problem, try to keep the anger from affecting your posture, your voice, and the content of what you say. If you want the other person to understand that the situation is making you angry, tell them so as clearly and as openly as you can. For example: *"I find that the situation makes me feel angry, and that makes it hard for me to think."*

Sometimes you may become so angry that you can't continue the discussion productively. A clear message to this effect may be appropriate. *"I'm getting so upset that I can't discuss this clearly right now. I'd like to take a breather and try again tomorrow."*

When you get angry during confrontations, how is this expressed? Do you express it in such a way that the other person becomes just as upset (either angry or anxious)?

_____

_____

How could you express it differently? Would this be helpful or would it just take the discussion away from the topic at hand?

_____

_____

_____

Wait Out Silences

Sometimes the other person will remain silent after you make your point. This may mean they are thinking. Good. Give them time. One of the ways that conflicts get out of hand is that people respond too quickly. Slower is often better.

One reason that silences *aren't* tolerated is the fear that, given time, the person will come up with a really good point. *"Better leap in there or they'll think of something I can't counter."* This invariably produces frustration in the person and makes an unproductive exchange more likely. If they can come up with a good point, let them. Part of the mission is to let them really *be there* in the exchange, including their inconvenient but valid points. Trying to shut them down won't work in the long run.

Some people, though, have learned that silence makes others nervous. They use silence as a control tool. If they don't react, the person confronting them may start to back down. Here's an example:

You: *". . . and so that's what I'd like to happen."*

Them: *Silence, which makes you nervous.*

You: *". . . if you'd be willing, that is . . ."*

Them: *Silence.*

You: *". . . I mean, I don't think it's too unreasonable . . ."*

Them: *Silence.*

You: *". . . is it? . . ."*

Them: *Silence.*

You: *". . . though I'd be happy even with a little bit . . ."*

Them: *Silence.*

You: *". . . or even if you'd just think about it . . ."*

You get the picture. The silent one doesn't even have to argue. All they have to do is wait and you will feel tempted to start backing down.

Instead of giving in to the anxiety that silence can produce, sit back and do your best to relax. Tolerate the silence. Wait for the other person to respond. Eventually they will. If the silence stretches on, you can ask for them to comment. *"I'd like to hear what you have to say about my request."* Don't change your position until the other person has stated theirs.

Is the other person involved in your issue silent during confrontations?

_____

Are they thinking during these silences, or do you think it's a control tool? If the latter, keep in mind that you might be wrong.

_____

_____

How could you respond if silences appear in the discussion you are planning?

_____

_____

Checkpoint: Things to Keep in Mind

After reading the recommendations above, ask yourself which ones address problems that you have had in past confrontations. If you overuse the passive, aggressive, or passive-aggressive style, which suggestions would best help you to maintain an assertive stance?

Then consider the situation you identified in chapter 15. Which points would be most helpful to remember during a confrontation on this issue? How could you use these ideas to keep the discussion on track? What is your strategy?

Point to remember: _____

Strategy: _____

_____

_____

Point to remember: _____

Strategy: _____

_____

_____

Point to remember: _____

Strategy: _____

_____

_____

After the Confrontation

Once the initial confrontation is over, there are still a few tasks to accomplish.

Reward Yourself

Even if the confrontation did not go perfectly, acknowledge that although it was difficult for you, you did it anyway. It can be easy to focus on the rough parts and forget to give yourself credit for your efforts. Instead, remind yourself what you have accomplished. You might also give yourself a treat for putting in the effort (perhaps just by taking some time to relax).

How will you acknowledge your efforts or reward yourself for facing this issue?

_____

_____

Monitor Results

Remember that if you want to be taken seriously, you have to live up to your stated consequences, positive and negative.

If things go well, comment on the fact. Ensure that the other person knows you appreciate and recognize their efforts. Don't be too picky. If your child performs the chore a minute after the deadline, consider the obligation met. Only make a comment if the lateness becomes greater and greater with time. If your spouse goes along with you to the opera but grumbles about it, do your best to ignore the grumbling and thank your spouse for the effort. If you promised a reward, make sure you deliver it.

If things do not go well, consider reminding the person about the negative consequences. Do not do so repeatedly. If you told your son that he could not watch television until the dishes were done, then allow him to make that choice without complaint. Do ensure, however, that the negative consequences occur. If you don't, the person you confronted will soon learn that you were bluffing and will not take you seriously in the future.

Did you put your confrontation plan into action? How did the discussion go?

_____

_____

_____

_____

What was the eventual outcome?

_____

_____

_____

Did you enact the "outcome" from your DESO script? How?

_____

_____

_____

POSTSCRIPT

BEING YOU

Congratulations! You have reached the end of this manual. Hopefully by now you have completed most of the exercises and have tried out some new assertiveness skills and strategies. Hopefully you have made some errors. Errors provide you with the opportunity to learn and adapt these skills to your own style. Hopefully, too, you have had a few successes. Success helps build motivation.

What *hasn't* happened?

Perhaps you have tended to overuse one of the less effective communication styles in the past—the passive, aggressive, or passive-aggressive style. If so, this style has become somewhat automatic for you. As automatic as, say, driving on the right-hand side of the road. If you were to move to England, you would find it hard to remember to drive on the left side, at least at first. Any new strategy—such as using the assertive style—will not be quite so automatic. You might know how to do it, but it won't happen all by itself. You'll still have to think about it.

Will assertiveness ever become second nature for you? Yes, it will gradually become easier. However:

- You will have to put up with a period of awkwardness while you get used to being more assertive. Just like learning to ride a bicycle, assertiveness feels awkward and unnatural until you are used to it.

- The only way to build assertive behavior as a habit is to practice. It is not enough to read the suggestions in this manual, or even to carry out a few experiments in your life. You will need to continue practicing. For a long while your first impulse will be to react with the style you are most accustomed to using. It will take effort to catch yourself, think, and use an assertive response instead.

- Assertiveness may *never* be as easy as aggression or passive avoidance. Assertiveness always requires that we think about what we believe and strive to hear what the other person is saying. Although this gets easier with practice, running away or behaving aggressively may always be easier. Assertiveness requires that we *be there*: that we use our minds and open our hearts. That's not always easy to do.

Why put in the effort? Simple. It works.

You exist. You can pretend otherwise by trying to hide yourself or deny your uniqueness. You can strive to be a ghost, invisible to others. But you will be pretending. You do exist. You're there.

Others exist too. They have thoughts, ideas, and preferences. They are inconvenient at times. We can use aggression to try to impose our will on them, to wipe out the differences between us, and to make them think, act, and behave as we think they should. But we will fail. They're still there. Still different from us. Still unique.

Through assertiveness we develop contact with ourselves and with others. We become real human beings with real ideas, real differences . . . and real flaws. And we admit all of these things. We don't try to become someone else's mirror. We don't try to suppress someone else's uniqueness. We don't try to pretend that we're perfect. We become ourselves. We allow ourselves to *be there*.

It's a big task and it takes courage. By reading this manual and trying out some experiments, you have had the courage to take a great many of the steps. Recognize your courage.

The path, however, doesn't end here. The steps leading into our lives continue—with more practice, more effort, and more confidence. Enjoy the path. *Be there*.

ANNOTATED RESOURCE LIST

Alberti, Robert, and Michael Emmons. 1995. *Your Perfect Right: A Guide to Assertive Living,* 7th ed. San Luis Obispo, Calif.: Impact Publishers.

This excellent book has been around since 1970 and is regularly updated by the authors. Well organized and readable, it provides straightforward recommendations for assertive communication. The book is especially strong in its coverage of the beliefs and attitudes that hold people back from being more assertive. Highly recommended.

Bourne, Edmund. 1998. *Healing Fear: New Approaches to Overcoming Anxiety.* Oakland, Calif.: New Harbinger Publications.

Bourne offers a broad survey of strategies for the individual coping with excessive anxiety. Given that anxiety is a primary barrier to effective assertive behavior, those who have a lot of anxiety may find this book invaluable.

Bower, Sharon Anthony, and Gordon H Bower. 1991. *Asserting Yourself: A Practical Guide for Positive Change*, 2nd ed. Reading, Mass.: Addison-Wesley Publishing.

This is an excellent book on assertiveness. Bower and Bower emphasize practical suggestions for dealing with real-life situations. They include many sample interactions between people for illustration, plus a number of writing exercises to help you to relate the ideas to your own life. Bower and Bower also developed the DESO script technique discussed in this manual (called "DESC scripts" in their book) and give numerous examples of it in action.

Butler, Pamela E. 1992. *Self-Assertion for Women,* rev. ed. New York: HarperCollins.

Women's upbringing and socialization, expectations from others, and role pressures often contribute to difficulties developing and utilizing assertion skills. Butler's book focuses on these difficulties and provides concrete suggestions for women in the process of becoming more assertive.

Catalano, Ellen M. 1990. *Getting to Sleep.* Oakland, Calif.: New Harbinger Publications.

An excellent overview of the difficulties that can plague sleep, along with a collection of strategies designed to overcome them.

Davis, Martha, Elizabeth R. Eshelman, and Matthew McKay. 2000. *The Relaxation and Stress Reduction Workbook,* 5th ed. Oakland, Calif.: New Harbinger Publications.

Stress-related tension can be a significant barrier to assertive behavior. This book reviews many of the most important and well-documented strategies for managing stress. Those who find themselves tensing up at the thought of being assertive may benefit a great deal from the strategies these authors recommend.

Hays, Kate F. 1999. *Working It Out: Using Exercise in Psychotherapy.* Washington, D.C.: American Psychological Association.

Written mainly for therapists, this book reviews the abundant literature on the link between exercise and mental health. Hays includes chapters on the role of exercise in a variety of issues, including weight loss, overcoming trauma, managing anxiety, and coping with chronic pain.

Jakubowski, Patricia, and Arthur J. Lange. 1978. *The Assertive Option: Your Rights and Responsibilities.* Champaign, Ill: Research Press.

A good book on assertiveness interspersed with self-tests, practice exercises, and considerable analysis of the role of thought in assertive and non-assertive behavior. More detailed than some books on the subject, *The Assertive Option* is a good bet for those wanting to examine the issue in depth.

McKay, Matthew, Martha Davis, and Patrick Fanning. 1995. *Messages: The Communications Skills Book,* 2nd ed. Oakland, Calif.: New Harbinger Publications.

Messages is an excellent and wide-ranging resource on communication skills, including assertiveness. There are chapters on listening skills, negotiation, sexual communication, parent effectiveness, and public speaking. A good choice for those wishing to look beyond assertiveness to other aspects of interpersonal communication.

Potter-Efron, Ron. 1994. *Angry All the Time: An Emergency Guide to Anger Control.* Oakland, Calif.: New Harbinger Publications.

For some people anger and aggression spiral out of control into extremely destructive (and self-defeating) behavior. This guide is designed to help the individual with chronic anger intervene before behaving aggressively.

Potter-Efron, Ron, and Pat Potter-Efron. 1995. *Letting Go of Anger: The 10 Most Common Anger Styles and What To Do about Them*. Oakland, Calif.: New Harbinger Publications.

Anger can manifest itself in any number of ways. This guide discusses some of the more common styles and how they produce aggressive or passive-aggressive behavior. It then goes on to give specific strategies for intervening with each pattern.

Seligman, Martin E.P. 1991. *Learned Optimism: How To Change Your Mind and Your Life*. New York: A. A. Knopf.

A cognitive-behavioral approach to depression and the development of a more optimistic demeanor, by the author who developed the influential learned helplessness theory of depression.

Smith, Manuel J. 1975. *When I Say No, I Feel Guilty*. New York: Bantam.

A classic in the field of assertiveness training, this book holds up well twenty-five years later. Smith uses extended sample dialogues to illustrate his ideas and provides a number of specific communication strategies to use in difficult situations.

ASSERTIVENESS SCORECARDS

For you to become more assertive you will have to pay a great deal of attention to your difficult interactions with others. This will help you gain a clearer idea of the situations that are most challenging for you and the ways that you could approach these situations differently. Use the Assertiveness Scorecards on the following page to keep a record of each difficult or awkward interaction that you have as you work through this book. You have our permission to make as many photocopies of the Scorecard page as you wish. Each page has two Scorecards. Each Scorecard is used to record a separate interaction.

You don't need to record every conversation you have with other people, but do fill out a Scorecard in the following circumstances:

- If your encounter with the person turns out badly.

- If you believe that you behaved passively or aggressively rather than assertively.

- If you interact with an especially difficult person (no matter how well or badly it turned out).

- If you feel resentful, weak, disappointed, or guilty afterward.

Use one box for each encounter. Here's how to fill it out:

- **Date/Time/Place**: When and where did it happen?

- **Person/Situation**: Who were you talking to? About what?

- **Your Response**: What did you do or say? How did you act?

- **Assertive, Passive, Aggressive, or P/A?**: Use the definitions of assertive, passive, aggressive, and passive-aggressive (P/A) behavior from chapter 1. Pick the one that best describes your response.

- **How did it turn out?**: What was the outcome?

- **Feelings Afterward**: How did you feel? Satisfied, hurt, anxious, angry, resentful?

- **Alternative Response**: If you decide that you did not behave assertively, how could you have handled the situation differently?

Date: _____ Time: _____ Place: _____

Person/Situation: _____

_____

Your Response: _____

_____

Assertive, Passive, Aggressive, or P/A? _____

How did it turn out? _____

Feelings Afterward: _____

Alternative Response: _____

_____

_____

_____

Date: _____ Time: _____ Place: _____

Person/Situation: _____

_____

Your Response: _____

_____

Assertive, Passive, Aggressive, or P/A? _____

How did it turn out? _____

Feelings Afterward: _____

Alternative Response: _____

_____

_____

_____

Date: _____ Time: _____ Place: _____

Person/Situation: _____

_____

Your Response: _____

_____

Assertive, Passive, Aggressive, or P/A? _____

How did it turn out? _____

Feelings Afterward: _____

Alternative Response: _____

_____

_____

_____

Date: _____ Time: _____ Place: _____

Person/Situation: _____

_____

Your Response: _____

_____

Assertive, Passive, Aggressive, or P/A? _____

How did it turn out? _____

Feelings Afterward: _____

Alternative Response: _____

_____

_____

_____

More New Harbinger Titles

THE SHYNESS AND SOCIAL ANXIETY WORKBOOK

An intensive, self-directed program helps you improve communication skills and feel confident about new relationships and begin to live a life no longer controlled by fear and anxiety.   *Item SHYW $16.95*

TOXIC COWORKERS

This fascinating look at what underlies the variety of bizarre and annoying behavior that so many of us encounter on the job explains how to develop effective strategies for dealing with common personality traits and personality disorders.   *Item TOXC $13.95*

DANCING NAKED

Imaginative exercises help you embrace the uncertainties of today's job market and manage your career with confidence and maximum effectiveness. *Item DNCE $14.95*

MAKING HOPE HAPPEN

A powerful program shows you how to break old self-defeating habits, overcome roadblocks, and find new routes to your goals.   *Item HOPE $14.95*

WORKING ANGER

A step-by-step program designed to help anyone who has had trouble dealing with their own anger or other people's anger at work.   *Item WA $12.95*

DON'T TAKE IT PERSONALLY

Shows you how to depersonalize your responses to rejection, establish boundaries that protect you from hurt, and develop a new sense of self-acceptance and self-confidence.   *Item DOTA $15.95*

Call **toll-free 1-800-748-6273** to order. Have your Visa or Mastercard number ready. Or send a check for the titles you want to New Harbinger Publications, 5674 Shattuck Avenue, Oakland, CA 94609. Include $4.50 for the first book and 75¢ for each additional book to cover shipping and handling. (California residents please include appropriate sales tax.) Allow four to six weeks for delivery.

Prices subject to change without notice.

Some Other
New Harbinger Titles

Depressed and Anxious, Item 3635 $19.95

Angry All the Time, Item 3929 $13.95

Handbook of Clinical Psychopharmacology for Therapists, 4th edition, Item 3996 $55.95

Writing For Emotional Balance, Item 3821 $14.95

Surviving Your Borderline Parent, Item 3287 $14.95

When Anger Hurts, 2nd edition, Item 3449 $16.95

Calming Your Anxious Mind, Item 3384 $12.95

Ending the Depression Cycle, Item 3333 $17.95

Your Surviving Spirit, Item 3570 $18.95

Coping with Anxiety, Item 3201 $10.95

The Agoraphobia Workbook, Item 3236 $19.95

Loving the Self-Absorbed, Item 3546 $14.95

Transforming Anger, Item 352X $10.95

Don't Let Your Emotions Run Your Life, Item 3090 $17.95

Why Can't I Ever Be Good Enough, Item 3147 $13.95

Your Depression Map, Item 3007 $19.95

Successful Problem Solving, Item 3023 $17.95

Working with the Self-Absorbed, Item 2922 $14.95

The Procrastination Workbook, Item 2957 $17.95

Coping with Uncertainty, Item 2965 $11.95

The BDD Workbook, Item 2930 $18.95

You, Your Relationship, and Your ADD, Item 299X $17.95

The Stop Walking on Eggshells Workbook, Item 2760 $18.95

Conquer Your Critical Inner Voice, Item 2876 $15.95

The PTSD Workbook, Item 2825 $17.95

Hypnotize Yourself Out of Pain Now!, Item 2809 $14.95

The Depression Workbook, 2nd edition, Item 268X $19.95

Beating the Senior Blues, Item 2728 $17.95

Call **toll free, 1-800-748-6273,** or log on to our online bookstore at **www.newharbinger.com** to order. Have your Visa or Mastercard number ready. Or send a check for the titles you want to New Harbinger Publications, Inc., 5674 Shattuck Ave., Oakland, CA 94609. Include $4.50 for the first book and 75¢ for each additional book, to cover shipping and handling. (California residents please include appropriate sales tax.) Allow two to five weeks for delivery.

Prices subject to change without notice.